CONNOR McDAVID
HOCKEY'S NEXT GREAT ONE

ROB SORIA

TRIUMPH
BOOKS

This book is available in quantity at special discounts for your group or organization.
For further information contact:

Triumph Books LLC
814 North Franklin Street
Chicago, Illinois, 60610
Phone: (312) 337-0747
www.triumphbooks.com

Printed in the United States of America

ISBN: 978-1-62937-472-7

Content packaged by Alex Lubertozzi

All photos courtesy of AP Images

Contents

Introduction

When it comes to being a hockey fan, I count myself among the lucky ones. Even though I lived in the city of Edmonton during the 1980s and experienced firsthand what Wayne Gretzky and the Oilers were all about, it is next to impossible to put into words. Watching that collection of players go out and dominate on a night-in and night-out basis is something no one will ever have the privilege of witnessing again. There is a reason why they are among the most storied teams in NHL history. It was a special group of players who were led by an exceptional talent and individual.

As wonderful as the first 13 years of franchise history were, the following two-plus decades haven't been so kind. After winning five Stanley Cup championships in six trips to the finals and reaching the conference finals on two other occasions, Edmonton missed the playoffs in 15 of the next 22 seasons. In short, they went from the penthouse to the outhouse and appeared to be spinning their wheels. With a nine-year playoff drought staring them squarely in the face, this organization needed something to help them turn the tide, and that something came in the form of Connor McDavid.

For the second time in franchise history, the Oilers landed a player who will go down in hockey annals among the best to have ever played the game, and both times it came down to dumb luck. While there have always been a couple of so-called "stories" out there surrounding how Edmonton actually secured the rights to No. 99, at the end of the day, he fell into their lap because Indianapolis Racers owner Nelson Skalbania needed money. Peter Pocklington was in the right place at the right time, and it landed him and his hockey team a get-out-of-jail-free card.

With McDavid, it came down to what order a lottery blower pushed out some Ping-Pong balls. Not quite the same thing, but in some ways they are similar. Luck comes in all forms, shapes, and sizes. For a league that has arguably had four generational talents make their way through the ranks over the course of its history, the fact that two of them found their way to the Alberta capital in peculiar ways is rather astonishing. Think about it for a minute, to land both Gretzky and McDavid seems so farfetched that it's laughable. Yet here we are, and history could very well be repeating itself.

Despite following the club throughout their championship-winning years, I wasn't old enough or capable of properly chronicling what those Oilers teams and their captain accomplished during their historic run. Fast forward to the present day, and the outlet is now at my disposal, and I felt it was simply too good an opportunity to pass up. Having the wherewithal to draw on memories of this club's storied history and using it as a springboard to what the future could hold seemed like a natural fit. Add the potential similarities between Gretzky and McDavid, and this project essentially wrote itself.

Again, it's not every day that we get the chance to witness true greatness in the world of sport, and we are getting our second shot at it in Edmonton. From my standpoint, it is hard to compute that the Oilers have been a part of the NHL for nearly 40 years. The inaugural 1979–80 season was a long time ago, but for an old guy like me, the arrival of McDavid has brought all those memories back to the forefront. Those were special times in this city and ones that most Edmontonians took great pride in and still do to this day. The love for this team has never gone away, and it's arguably stronger than ever.

The problem is much of this fan base has yet to experience the feelings that come with repeated viewings of greatness, be it on the individual or team side of the equation. Some were given a sneak peek to the latter during the Oilers' surprise run to the 2006 Stanley Cup Finals. However, nothing has come close to the former since Gretzky's departure in the summer of 1988. But that is about to change in short order. Having already lived through it once, I can tell you there is nothing quite like it, and recognizing what you are watching makes it all the more extraordinary.

With that said, the key in all of this is to enjoy it while you can. It may seem a long way away, but just as in our day-to-day existence, time goes by far more quickly than we think it does. When it comes to Connor McDavid and the Oilers of today, the sole focus should be on soaking up as much of the here and now as possible. There is no question the future is bright, but a situation such as this should be cherished, as a player of this stature is unlikely to ever call Edmonton home again. So do yourself a favour, Oilers nation, count your lucky stars and get prepared to be wowed. ■

Edmonton Oilers' captain Connor McDavid warms up before a preseason game in October 2016 at Rogers Place.

Draft Lottery

The phrase "generational talent" is not used very often in hockey circles, and there's a good reason. Over the course of the last 50-plus years, there has been a grand total of three men who managed to find their way onto said list: Bobby Orr, Wayne Gretzky, and Mario Lemieux. Not surprisingly, it is a rare occasion when a kid coming out of junior hockey has that tag tied to his name. For a long time, that list included only the names of Eric Lindros and Sidney Crosby, but that changed at the 2015 National Hockey League Entry Draft.

Connor McDavid was not the first, nor will he be the last, player to be viewed as a special talent while in minor hockey. After all, it is not uncommon to see a talented player look as though he belongs on another level at a young age. However, when a 14- to 15-year-old goes out and posts totals of 79 goals, 130 assists, and 209 points in 88 games at the minor midget level, it is next to impossible to ignore. That is exactly what McDavid did during the 2011–12 campaign with the Toronto Marlboros, which led to him being named the Greater Toronto Hockey League's Player of the Year.

Not surprisingly, Hockey Canada also tagged him with "Exceptional Player" status, granting him the privilege of entering the Ontario Hockey League Draft a year early. While other 15-year-olds had been given similar treatment, most notably New York Islanders forward John Taveras and Florida Panthers defenceman Aaron Ekblad, the Richmond Hill native had whispers of potential greatness surrounding him (a "generational talent" if you will).

Perhaps the simplest and most accurate scouting report of McDavid came courtesy of TSN Director of Scouting Craig Button leading up the 2015 draft: "Two words: unprecedented speed. Skating speed, hand quickness, and mental processing that he executes simultaneously to threaten defenders and create opportunities. He would be the first pick in every draft since Sidney Crosby in 2005, perhaps even in Crosby's draft year."

The Erie Otters used their good fortune to select McDavid with the first pick of the OHL Draft, and the rest is history. Over the course of his three seasons with the Otters, he not only scored at a ridiculous clip (97 goals, 188 assists, and 285 points in 166 games) but helped transform Erie from one of the worst teams in the league to one of its best. As impressive as his performance was—one that made him the most decorated player in league history—it was McDavid's play during the 2015 playoffs that was arguably the high point of his junior career and left all 30 NHL organizations salivating at what the future might hold.

After having his season interrupted due to a broken hand he suffered punching the end boards during a fight with Mississauga Steelheads captain Bryson Cianfrone in mid-November, McDavid elevated his

In three seasons with the OHL's Erie Otters, Connor McDavid scored 97 goals and added another 188 assists in just 166 games. Although he was sidelined briefly with a broken hand in November 2014, he would go on to be the No. 1 overall pick in the 2015 NHL Entry Draft.

"Two words: unprecedented speed…He would be the first pick in every draft since Sidney Crosby in 2005, perhaps even in [2005]." —Craig Button

play down the stretch and in the postseason. While Erie ultimately fell in five games to a far superior Oshawa Generals side in the league final, McDavid put his team on his back throughout the postseason. Game in and game out, it was one breathtaking rush after another and there was seemingly nothing the opposition could do about it.

The numbers were absolutely jaw-dropping: 21 goals and 49 points in 20 games. And if you had the pleasure of watching the Otters during their playoff push, you know just how dominant No. 97 was. There was the unforgettable five-goal night against the perennial powerhouse London Knights in Game 2 of the second round, a series sweep in which McDavid had 14 points. He was arguably even better against the Sault Ste. Marie Greyhounds in Round 3, with 20 points in six games, including a pair of five-point efforts—the last of which came in the series clincher.

The funny thing is, in between those two series, the NHL held their now annual Draft Lottery to see who would luck into getting the first overall selection in the 2015 Entry Draft. In the midst of what turned out to be a 10-game stretch in which McDavid scored 17 times and chipped in with another 17 helpers, nearly half the league's franchises couldn't help but wonder how their lot in life might change if the balls bounced their way on

April 18, 2016. No matter how things played out, only one would come away from this exercise with a smile on its face, and that one was none other than Edmonton.

That's right, instead of the last-place Buffalo Sabres, who blatantly tanked in 2014–15 in hopes of improving their chances in the lottery, or to the team most media types were openly rooting for leading up to the festivities, the Toronto Maple Leafs, the game's next great talent was essentially gifted to the franchise that had picked first in three consecutive years from 2010 to 2012. While those drafts produced what looked to be a fairly substantial haul in Taylor Hall, Ryan Nugent-Hopkins, and Nail Yakupov, this was on a completely different level. In a split second, the hockey world was turned upside down.

While Edmonton did not actually win the lottery in 2011 (the New Jersey Devils did but were only able to move up a maximum of four spots, going from eighth to fourth, in the draft order), this marked the third time in six years they did, and fourth time they would have the No. 1 pick. Hence, it was no real surprise to hear the outcry from both those inside the game and fan bases across the league. With their recent history being what it was and just an 11.5 percent chance of success this time around, the Oilers logo was the one few expected Deputy Commissioner Bill Daly

McDavid (97) celebrates with Otters teammates after their Game 3 victory over the Sault Ste. Marie Greyhounds in the OHL Western Conference Finals on April 26, 2015. McDavid was unstoppable in the playoffs, scoring 21 goals and 49 points in 20 games, including 20 points in six games against the Greyhounds.

to reveal as the evening's big winner. And yet there it was, in all its glory, for all to see.

Despite their recent struggles, we are talking about one of the NHL's most storied franchises and the place the greatest player of all-time called home for the prime years of his career. While having a kid with McDavid's skillset and potential greatness wind up in Edmonton may not seem like an ideal fit for the league to take full advantage of his marketability and help grow the game's reach, there is something to be said for having "the Next One" do his thing in the old stomping grounds of "the Great One"… as does having him in a Canadian market that both worships the game and its history.

Is it understandable that Edmonton was the place few wanted to see McDavid end up? Of course, but in the end, it actually turned out to be one of the better landing spots for him. Don't agree? Well, something tells me Sidney Crosby would have an idea or two about what the kid was about to experience, and he had the following to say to the *Pittsburgh Tribune-Review*'s Josh Yohe when asked about his thoughts on the youngster heading to the Alberta capital:

The great thing for him is that they have a lot of young guys there already. That's a big thing for him. It's not like he's going to an older team or anything like that. He'll be able to grow with those guys. They have a ton of young talent there already, so it should be a good thing for him to be there. ■

McDavid at a press conference in Toronto on Saturday, April 18, 2015. The Edmonton Oilers won the NHL draft lottery and the right to select McDavid with the first pick in the 2015 NHL Entry Draft.

McDavid chats with Edmonton's VP of Hockey Operations Craig MacTavish after being chosen first overall by the Oilers in the NHL Entry Draft, June 26, 2015, in Sunrise, Florida.

McDavid sports his new No. 97 Oilers jersey flanked by team owner Daryl Katz's son Harrison (left) and Craig MacTavish, after being chosen first overall by the Edmonton Oilers in the 2015 NHL Entry Draft.

Scoring Race

While he may not yet be a member of the Edmonton Oilers, Connor McDavid has already taken Oilers nation by storm. Ever since this organization had the good fortune of winning the NHL Draft Lottery, it has become next to impossible to find a fan of the Orange and Blue who wants to focus on anything but the future of their beloved hockey team.

Despite another four-point effort from the soon-to-be first overall pick during Game 4 of the Ontario Hockey League Final between the Erie Otters and Oshawa Generals on Wednesday night, the Otters dropped a 6–5 overtime decision and are now just one defeat away from seeing their season end before reaching the 2015 Memorial Cup. With that said, McDavid has certainly delivered the goods in his junior hockey swan song.

After yesterday's goal and three-assist performance against the Generals, the absurdly talented youngster has now scored 21 times and chipped in with 28 helpers in just 19 postseason appearances. To put that into perspective, Oshawa's Michael Dal Colle currently sits second in playoff scoring with 29 points in 20 games played. In other words, this kid is on a completely different plane, and everyone knows it.

As if expectations were not going to be crazy enough, the moment Wayne Gretzky came out and said, "He's as good as I've seen in the last 30 years,"

was the very moment this thing went in an altogether different direction. While the common hockey fan generally uses Sidney Crosby as a potential comparable for the 2015 OHL Player of the Year, No. 99's comments suggest the better comparison may very well be that other guy who played for the Pittsburgh Penguins all those years ago and wore No. 66 on his back.

With all due respect to Mr. Crosby, as great a career as he has been able to put together, he is nowhere near the offensive machine that Mario Lemieux was during his 17 years in the National Hockey League. There is no question today's game is far more structured and played by far better athletes than it was three decades ago, but the numbers Gretzky and Lemieux consistently produced throughout their careers speak for themselves.

If McDavid proves to be as good as advertised and needs only a minimal amount of time to adjust to the pro game, would it really be so far-fetched to expect him to finish among the league's leading scorers in his rookie season? While some might suggest that could be a bit of a stretch, let us not forget that Jamie Benn led the National Hockey League in scoring in 2014–15 with a grand total of 87 points.

Now there certainly is a difference between scoring at a 2.55-PPG clip in the OHL and putting up points on a nightly basis in the NHL during an

Connor McDavid (17) scores for Team Canada against Denmark's goalie Georg Sorensen during quarterfinal action at the World Junior Hockey Championships in Toronto on January 2, 2015.

82-game grind. No one is suggesting he is going to produce at that same rate in the pros. However, to think McDavid will not be able to average somewhere in the neighbourhood of a point per game playing alongside the likes of talented youngsters like Leon Draisaitl, Jordan Eberle, Taylor Hall, Ryan Nugent-Hopkins, and Nail Yakupov would seem extremely unlikely.

Will he have to deal with his fair share of growing pains over the course of his rookie campaign? Most certainly, but you can pretty much bank on him delivering a handful of memorable performances that will leave hockey fans across the league shaking their heads in disbelief and allow him to pad his stats in the process. At 18 years of age, McDavid should not be expected to carry this team to the promised land, but thinking he could put up some eye-popping totals in what has correctly been branded as a "3-2 league" by Los Angeles Kings bench boss Darryl Sutter, is more than reasonable.

After all, we are talking about a generational talent, and those players tend to live up to their billing—especially when we are talking about the National Hockey League. This kid is going to be pretty darn special, and in my mind, if he is given the chance to play alongside Taylor Hall and the two remain relatively healthy, there is absolutely no reason to think Connor McDavid cannot push the 80-point mark during his first season. It might sound like a bit much, but when it comes to No. 97 and what he might accomplish, the sky truly is the limit. ■

This article was adapted from a piece that originally appeared at The Hockey Writers (copyright © May 14, 2015) and is used with permission.

McDavid celebrates his goal against Denmark.

The McDavid Era

For most Canadian sports fans, July 1 is viewed as a special day on the calendar. Not only is it the day people across Canada are given the opportunity to celebrate how wonderful this country is, it also marks the opening day of free agency in the National Hockey League. With that said, yesterday was an extra special day for the Edmonton Oilers and their long-suffering fan base.

While Peter Chiarelli was doing his best to try and upgrade his current roster for the 2015–16 campaign via free agency, the organization's new prized pupil took to the ice for the first time as an NHL player. As thrilled as fans were to see the club's general manager aggressively pursue and sign unrestricted free agent defenceman Andrej Sekera and centre Mark Letestu to multi-year deals on Wednesday morning, the real news of the day was the arrival of Connor McDavid.

As if his presence weren't already enough, the fact that both Leon Draisaitl and Darnell Nurse were also at the same camp signalled a turning point of sorts for this franchise. When asked how he felt about having all three youngsters at the same development camp, Chiarelli's response of, "It makes you tingle," shows the importance of the moment has not been lost on those who are now running the show.

Whether you want to believe it or not, there is a good chance that the Oilers' current setup will eventually turn into something special. While the "new regime" has done their best to keep expectations in check for both the club and its new superstar player, the writing is on the wall. To their credit, we have not heard a single peep from any prominent figure inside the organization on what the future might hold, and it is a refreshing change of pace.

Despite large chunks of the national media and a variety of fan bases across the league going on at great length about how "unhappy" the former Erie Otters star forward looked with having to make his way to the city of Edmonton, the kid has done his best to defuse the situation. And yet these silly rumours continue to make the rounds. Unfortunately, far too many are confusing surprise with disappointment.

Whether it was just a matter of seizing the moment to get his point across or simply a coincidence, McDavid decided to take it a step further yesterday afternoon. After being asked how things went during his first day of camp, the youngster delivered the following little nugget to a horde of local scribes following his first official on-ice session as a member of the Orange and Blue.

"Today was a lot of fun," said McDavid. "The fitness testing wasn't a whole lot of fun, but it was really cool to throw on the Oilers gear, the gear that I want to play the rest of my life wearing. It was very special to put on and to step onto Rexall…with all the history…it was a lot of fun."

Edmonton Oilers No. 1 overall pick Connor McDavid takes part in team orientation camp in Edmonton on July 1, 2015.

Despite knowing all-too-well that expectations would be through the roof, especially playing in one of the league's most rabid hockey markets, McDavid wasted no time in trying to calm the waters. For him to come out and handle the situation in the manner he did was awfully impressive and shows a maturity well beyond his years. Clearly, this kid understands how this media thing works and just how important stopping a non-story in its tracks can be.

In a span of roughly 30 seconds, the youngster managed to not only put the Oilers fan base at ease but also throw a wrench into the plans of media types everywhere who were counting on running with this angle for the foreseeable future. While certainly a tough break for those who enjoy writing splashy headlines, it was an absolute godsend for this hockey club. The last thing this team needed heading into 2015–16 was a parade of questions surrounding the supposed unhappiness of their new star pupil and yesterday all but ensured that would not happen.

No matter how you look at it, this was a momentous occasion of sorts for the Edmonton Oilers—a turning of the page, if you will. For the first time in ages, this franchise has become relevant again and looks to finally be headed in the right direction. There is no question the past decade has been rough on the organization, its players, and their fans, but it appears as though the light at the end of the tunnel has finally started to shine through the cracks.

The people of Edmonton were fortunate enough to witness true greatness on a nightly basis from 1978 to 1988, thanks to a kid by the name of Wayne Gretzky. But they've had little else to get excited about over the past 25 or so years. Well, that is about to change, and let's hope disgruntled hockey fans everywhere can put aside their disappointment with the city Connor McDavid ultimately ended up in and simply enjoy what should turn out to be one heck of a ride. ∎

This article was adapted from a piece that originally appeared at The Hockey Writers (copyright © July 2, 2015) and is used with permission.

McDavid looks on during orientation camp.

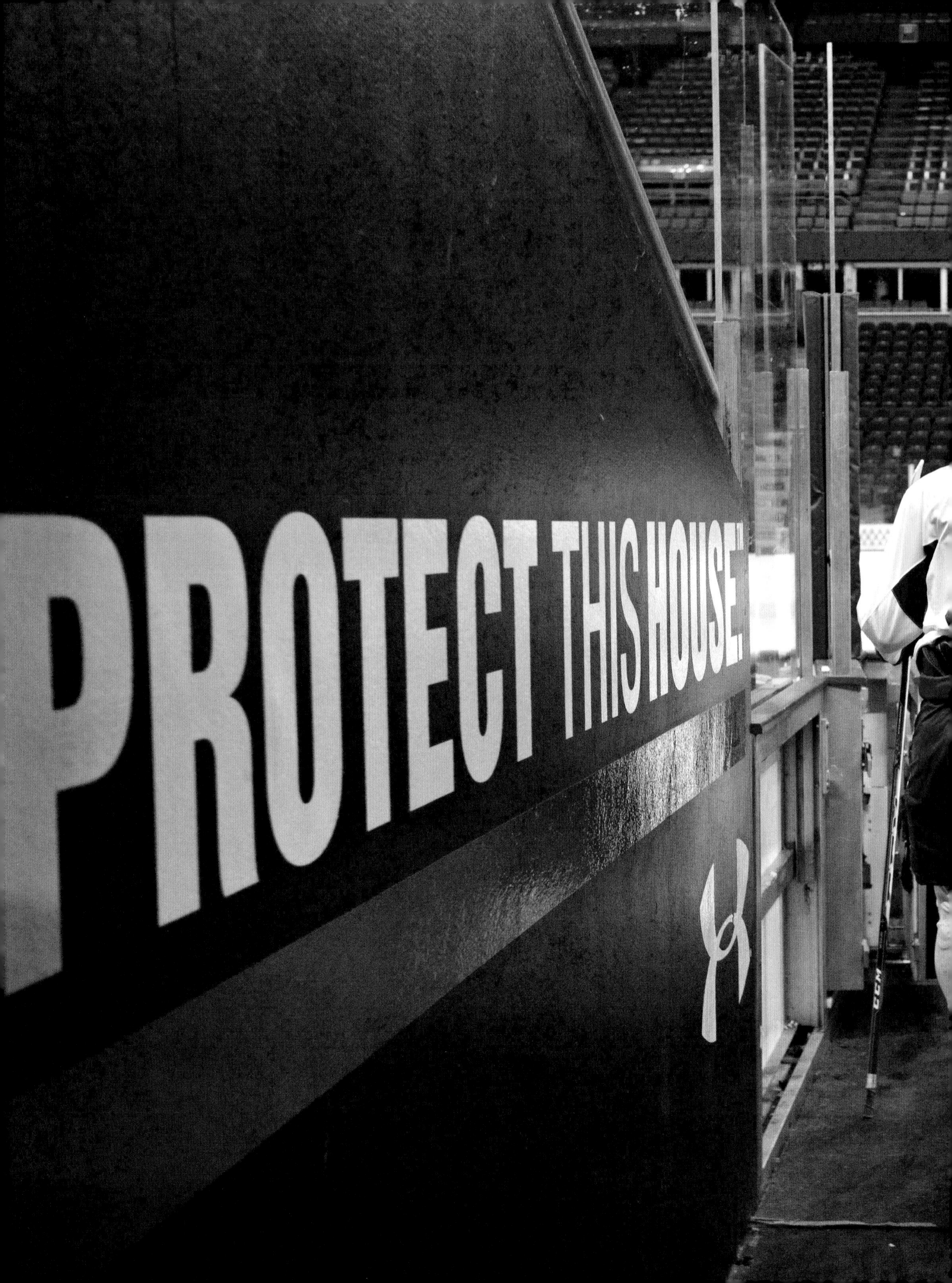
PROTECT THIS HOUSE.™

McDavid walks out onto the ice for the first time at Rexall Place.

Opening Night Jitters

With the Edmonton Oilers set to open their 2015–16 campaign on a three-game road trip and playing five of the first six away from Rexall Place, the chances of Connor McDavid getting off to a quick start in his NHL career seemed highly unlikely. The combination of still getting accustomed to the pro game and new teammates, coupled with facing three of the better teams in the Western Conference would certainly make life tough for No. 97 and company out of the gate.

The St. Louis Blues held up their end of the bargain in the season opener, keeping the young phenom and the rest of the Oilers in check en route to a 3–1 victory. While going pointless in his debut was never supposed to be part of the script, the fact of the matter is, all that was secondary. As spectacular as going out and having a night to remember might have been, it likely would not have changed much of anything about the moment.

How so, you ask? Well, the first game of any professional athlete's career isn't supposed to be about making a splash, it's about celebrating an achievement. Even for a player as highly touted as McDavid, the countless hours of work and sacrifices that were made in order to get to this point cannot be overstated. Chances are the magnitude of the moment didn't hit

home until he stepped out onto that sheet of ice for the first time and realized his dream of playing in the NHL had come true. Safe to say the so-called butterflies were likely working overtime.

As if the occasion weren't already intense enough, Todd McLellan wasted no time in throwing his star pupil to the wolves, having him centre Anton Slepyshev and Taylor Hall. So much for breaking the kid in slowly. Again, while his evening did not go as he had envisioned, the opener was by no means a complete write-off for the No. 1 pick in the 2015 Entry Draft. In fact, one could argue it gave us an early glimpse into the kind of game McDavid brings to the table on a nightly basis.

After being kept relatively quiet through the opening 40 minutes of play, he started showing signs of life early in the third and registered his only two shots of the game. McDavid sent a buzz through the crowd courtesy of his one-on-two rush, in which he blew past the Blues' top pairing of Jay Bouwmeester and Alex Pietrangelo before forcing Brian Elliott into making a nifty little stop with the game still tied. And then he followed it up with another glorious chance, but Elliott was once again up to the task.

A tough break to be sure, and when asked about it during postgame interviews, the rookie centre

The Oilers' Connor McDavid makes his NHL debut versus the St. Louis Blues on October 8, 2015, in St. Louis.

didn't mince words. "I did some good stuff, did some bad stuff," McDavid said. "I had a couple chances that I need to score on." No excuses, just an honest assessment from a player who understands his role. Disappointment aside, it was a performance that did not go unnoticed to those inside the St. Louis dressing room.

"That McDavid's going to be a good player," Pietrangelo said. "He's a special talent … pretty impressed." While it's one thing for the opposing team's head coach to heap praises on a rookie in this kind of situation, it's quite another hearing it come out of a Canadian Olympian and two-time Second-Team All-Star defencemen after a single viewing, albeit up close and personal.

Taking all of that into consideration, the most pleasant surprise of the night revolved around the Richmond native's overall game. As expected, he was a complete and utter train wreck in the faceoff circle, but what wasn't expected was just how good his two-way game is. From his first shift to his last, McDavid appeared to be every bit as engaged in his own end of the rink as he was in the offensive zone. Time and time again we saw him stay with his man deep into the Oilers end and not take shortcuts of any kind.

Not exactly a common characteristic for an elite offensive talent to have, and certainly not the norm for a kid playing the first game of his pro career. Despite all the hype surrounding his arrival on the scene and potential impact on the roster, the fact that McDavid went out of his way to focus on his two-way game speaks volumes. Let's not forget, McLellan had been preaching defensive zone accountability from the moment training camp opened, as the Oilers have traditionally struggled with the finer points of the game in recent years.

In his rookie debut, McDavid didn't manage to dent the scoresheet but impressed nonetheless.

As the veteran journalist and current Sportsnet contributor Mark Spector aptly noted at the time, "McDavid does not play with a score-or-be-scored-on mentality. That puts McDavid well ahead on the learning curve in a league where every successful coach or top scorer will admit that offence is created only when the game is played properly in the defensive zone." Truer words have not been spoken, and his efforts did not go unnoticed by those in his own dressing room.

"I see a guy who's coming back. He's not cheating," said veteran winger Matt Hendricks. "The best players in the league play that way, and they end up winning Cups." While the individual admiration and accolades are all well and good, the two things that have driven McDavid from a very young age are winning and a desire to be the best. For the truly elite athlete, the two go hand and hand. Without team success, everything else becomes secondary.

"I thought his best period was the third," McLellan said. "When we needed him to be an offensive threat, he was, and he almost scored. We're talking 60 minutes into a 15- or 20-year career. He's going to get a lot better as time goes on." ■

McDavid had two shots on goal during the third period of the Oilers' 3–1 loss to the Blues.

McDavid (97) sits on the bench with teammates during the first period of a game against the Dallas Stars on October 13, 2015, in Dallas.

We Have Contact

After watching their team start the 2015–16 season with four consecutive losses, fans of the Edmonton Oilers could not help but wonder what was going on. Despite having the good fortune of Connor McDavid fall into their lap via the NHL Draft Lottery, winning hockey games was still proving to be quite a chore. While the schedule maker did them no favours, with games against the Nashville Predators and Dallas Stars, and a pair of dates versus the St. Louis Blues (home and away) to kick off their campaign, the fact that their new prized possession had yet to deliver that signature performance had much of Oilers nation on edge.

Through the first four games of his rookie season, McDavid had scored a single goal on just seven shots and posted a rather unflattering dash-5 under the plus/minus category. Obviously, it was not the greatest of starts, but a handful of games do not make a season. While keeping the kid off the scoresheet during his time in the OHL was a near impossible task, things aren't quite so easy at this level. No matter how good the player, today's NHL coach can find a way to quiet anyone for short periods of time.

So it was always a matter of time before McDavid turned in a so-called breakout performance and Edmonton won its first game of the year. Enter a date

with the Calgary Flames, and on *Hockey Night in Canada* to boot. Be it the seemingly weekly tradition of the Montreal Canadiens and Toronto Maple Leafs being featured in the early game or one of the Flames, Oilers, or Vancouver Canucks bringing it home in the second half doubleheader, there is something extra special about being on the tube from coast to coast on Saturday night.

Being the one who never seems to shy away from the spotlight, it seemed almost fitting for McDavid to deliver that signature performance in the Battle of Alberta, and on *HNIC*. After both he and his teammates struggled mightily to find their way to start the year, everything started to click against the Flames, and there was nothing Bob Hartley's crew could do to stop it. In the blink of an eye, an offence that had scored a total five goals over their previous five games could suddenly do no wrong in Calgary, and No. 97 was leading the charge.

"Best game yet, I think, from Connor," Todd McLellan said. "He made an impact throughout the night. Had an impact on the scoresheet, probably could've had more of an impact there even with some of the chances he had. I thought he finally gave himself permission to go. Sometimes you have to do that to get after it. As a young player, you don't have to give way to

Connor McDavid during his breakout performance in Calgary on October 17, 2015, in which he scored two goals and an assist to lead the Oilers past the Flames 5–2.

McDavid (97) celebrates one of his two goals against Calgary with teammate Eric Gryba (62), during the third period.

the veterans all the time. You're allowed to go out and take charge, and I thought he did that tonight."

The first two-goal game of his career and a stunning behind-the-back pass to start a tic-tac-toe with Benoit Pouliot and Nail Yakupov helped cap off a three-point effort, and the performance the entire hockey world was waiting for. While the 5–2 win was not all on McDavid, as Cam Talbot was rock-solid in between the pipes and Taylor Hall chipped in with three points of his own, there was no questioning who the star of the show was.

"He was great," Hall said. "He's got all the tools to take over games, and that's what he did tonight, and it was fun. I hope he gets a lot of confidence from that game because that's a tough building to come in and play and a really good road game for our team." Be it the pressure of having to deliver that signature performance no longer on his shoulders or the team actually ending up on the right side of a final score for the first time, that performance would trigger a seven-game stretch in which McDavid started to become a force on an almost shift-to-shift basis.

Over the course of the next two weeks, the Richmond native would pick up a point in each and every one of the Oilers games, and the club started to pick up points in the standings with some regularity. Edmonton followed up their 0–4 start with a solid 4–3 mark and only lost by more than a goal on one occasion, a 7–4 beatdown courtesy of Alex Ovechkin and the Washington Capitals. McDavid was productive throughout the run, scoring four times and chipping in with six assists, and his ice-time was starting to climb accordingly.

While he had previously been seeing anywhere from 16 to 18 minutes of ice on most nights, McLellan decided to up the ante and loosen the reins a little. So much so that McDavid was now being asked to play

north of 20 minutes on a nightly basis, and the extra workload seemed to push him to be even better. As his comfort level grew with both Pouliot and Yakupov, he started to look for open space without the puck and allow his wingers the opportunity to get him the puck in full stride and attack opposing defenders at top speed.

With this latest wrinkle now a regular occurrence and the club fighting the injury bug, Edmonton decided to recall Leon Draisaitl from the AHL and slot him on a line next to Hall and Ryan Nugent-Hopkins. With the McDavid trio starting to find some chemistry, the hope was that bringing the hulking German back into the picture would finally give the Oilers a semblance of two scoring lines. Ironically enough, the first test would come against the hottest team in the league, as the Montreal Canadiens and Carey Price paid their final visit to Rexall Place.

With the Habs coming in with a league-best 9–1 record, falling behind by three goals midway through the first and carrying a two-goal deficit into the second intermission was far from an ideal situation. In the end, it would be a dead tired Draisaitl who would be the one to play the role of hero, scoring the winner late in the final frame to cap off a three-point effort and help secure a thrilling 4–3 come-from-behind victory for the home side.

"That was unbelievable. We are all really happy for him," McDavid said. "That was pretty special. This feels really good. Obviously, that is the NHL's best team over there, and it feels pretty special to come back like that against them." With that said, were it not for a pair of brilliant plays from No. 97 early in the third, chances are the tide never turns and the Habs leave Rexall with two points firmly planted in their back pocket.

While his breathtaking end-to-end rush led directly to Brandon Davidson's power play blast that

McDavid gets mobbed by Andrew Ference (21) and Benoit Pouliot (67) after his goal against the Detroit Red Wings on October 21, 2015, in Edmonton.

cut the deficit to one, it was his sublime work on Pouliot's game-tying marker that left fans shaking their collective heads in disbelief. In what was a blink of an eye, McDavid managed to outwork P.K. Subban along the sideboards for a loose puck and promptly chip it past an oncoming Andrei Markov, all in one motion, to spring his linemate for a clear-cut breakaway. It was poetry in motion and something not seen in this neck of the woods since the days of No. 99.

Despite being the one who ultimately ended up paying for the kid's handiwork, the Canadiens' star netminder had nothing but praise and admiration for the young phenom. "McDavid is a dynamic player," Price said. "There is no question he's going to be an excellent addition to this league. He's exciting to watch, his talent is really outstanding. I'm really happy for the Oilers fans. They're going to be able to watch that for the next 15 to 20 years." ∎

McDavid in action against the Calgary Flames.

McDavid on offence in the first
two-goal game of his NHL career.

Disaster Strikes Oilers, McDavid, and NHL

After years of successfully putting together rosters that were just bad enough to ensure they would either be near or at the very top of every NHL Entry Draft since 2010, the Edmonton Oilers hit the jackpot in spring 2015 when Connor McDavid fell into their lap. While the other 29 organizations in the league and their collective fan bases were understandably disgusted with the outcome of last April's Draft Lottery, no hockey fan could have been happy with how things played out during the Oilers' 4–2 victory over the visiting Philadelphia Flyers at Rexall Place on November 3, 2015.

Injuries are part of the game, and while every team has to deal with them, no one likes to see the most talented players in the league miss extended periods of time. After watching McDavid crash into the end boards behind the Flyers net and pick himself up off the ice in the manner he did, following an ugly collision with defencemen Michael Del Zotto and Brandon Manning late in the second period, the writing was on the wall.

There are those who will try and argue it was a dirty play, but it was nothing of the sort. Yes, there was contact, but that is part of the game. Add to that the fact that McDavid was absolutely flying down the wing and appeared to catch a rut in the ice just as Manning made contact, and there was simply no way to avoid a major crash into the end boards. Watching the kid skate off the ice, favouring his shoulder and not moving his arm at all, told us all we needed to know.

To his credit, head coach Todd McLellan did not mince words during his postgame interview when asked about the status of his young phenom. "He's got an upper-body injury that is going to keep him out long-term and he is being evaluated right now by the doctors." Cut and dry, and to the point. While the Oilers may have been able to come back and eke out another victory—thanks in large part to another three-point effort from the suddenly red-hot Taylor Hall—celebrations were at a minimum across Oilers nation.

Be it a string of bad luck or perhaps karma for having so many No. 1 picks, it does seem a little ridiculous that almost every one of Edmonton's skilled youngsters have suffered major setbacks at one point or another since entering the league. Outside of Nail Yakupov, who has managed to stay away from the injury bug to this point in his career, the trio of Jordan Eberle, Hall, and Ryan Nugent-Hopkins have not been so fortunate. All three missed significant time, and with McDavid joining the club, it does feel like an endless carousel of sorts with this group.

Connor McDavid in the second period of the Edmonton Oilers' game against the Philadelphia Flyers on November 3, 2015.

While it does appear as though Eberle will be making his season's debut in the near future—most likely on Friday night against Sidney Crosby and the Pittsburgh Penguins—the loss of No. 97 creates a massive hole on this roster. Outside of Nugent-Hopkins, this team has nothing resembling a first- or second-line centre who could slide into McDavid's spot, and it will make life next to impossible for this group. And, no, using Leon Draisaitl in said role would not be a good idea at this time.

There is no question the Oilers will have their work cut out for them with their prized pupil unable to suit up for the foreseeable future, but the injury could not have come at a worse possible moment for the NHL. It's no secret that having McDavid wind up in Edmonton was not exactly the league's preferred destination for the future face of the game, but those are the cards they were dealt. Not an ideal situation but one that was far from unmanageable.

With the schedule being laid out in the manner it was, November and December were supposed to be his time to shine in the States. Unfortunately, that will no longer be the case. Safe to say Gary Bettman and company are not happy campers this morning, and it's hard to blame them. Just take a peek at the Oilers upcoming schedule, and you will quickly see how McDavid's injury has thrown a wrench in the league's upcoming schedule.

Perhaps it was just a coincidence, but over the next six weeks, Edmonton will be paying visits to the Anaheim Ducks, Arizona Coyotes, Boston Bruins, Carolina Hurricanes, Chicago Blackhawks (twice), Colorado Avalanche, Detroit Red Wings, Los Angeles Kings, New York Rangers, Pittsburgh Penguins, and Washington Capitals. Can you say "opportunity missed"?

And that doesn't even take into consideration the Oilers' lone trip to the Air Canada Centre in 2015–16 on November 30 to face off against the Toronto Maple Leafs, which would have been a guaranteed whirlwind for the Richmond Hill native and a media blitz, to be sure. Instead, we are left with the very real possibility that

Edmonton Oilers general manager Peter Chiarelli updates the press on injured Oilers rookie star Connor McDavid on November 4, 2015, the day after McDavid suffered a broken collarbone.

McDavid is all but guaranteed to miss a large chunk of what was supposed to be a rookie campaign for the ages.

With that in mind, the real downer in all of this is for the kid himself—something that was not lost on fellow youngster and former first overall pick Nugent-Hopkins. "You feel bad for Connor," he said. "It has been a long process getting to this point, then for something like that to happen was an unfortunate play.

You don't want to see anybody go into the boards with a couple of guys riding him. It was definitely tough to watch. He's already become a big part of our team. It's a loss in that sense, but we all just want him to know he has our support." ■

This article was adapted from a piece that originally appeared at The Hockey Writers (copyright © November 4, 2015) and is used with permission.

McDavid looks to score in the first period of the Oilers' 4–2 win over the Flyers. After suffering an injury in the second period, McDavid would miss the next three months of his rookie season.

Oilers Will Be in Tough Spot With or Without No. 97

Considering the Edmonton Oilers closed out 2015 with just one victory in their last eight games and are currently riding a four-game losing skid, one would think this group was due for some good fortune to kick off 2016. Something tells me having Connor McDavid return to practice for the first time since breaking his collarbone in early November against the Philadelphia Flyers would certainly qualify.

While Oilers nation has been buzzing since news of McDavid's inclusion in the club's New Year's Day practice hit social media, fans would be wise to keep their expectations in check when it comes to the rookie sensation. There is no question his return will instantly make this lineup better, but that does not necessarily mean it will translate into more wins for Todd McLellan's crew. With that said, it will at least give them a puncher's chance.

Bringing McDavid back into the fold will add some much-needed scoring depth up front and potentially spark what has truly been an awful power play over the last number of weeks. Add to that a much easier schedule over the next couple of months, and things should start to improve in the Alberta capital. After all, is there anyone who follows this team who doesn't want to see what a potential duo of Jordan Eberle and McDavid might deliver on a nightly basis? My guess is the answer to that question is a resounding no.

The next two months will be crucial in determining what direction Peter Chiarelli ultimately goes when it comes to addressing this roster in the summer. Be it finding out if there is a special chemistry waiting to be discovered between the likes of Eberle and McDavid or seeing where Nail Yakupov and perhaps even Zach Kassian fit. The coming weeks are essentially a trial run for this head coach to figure out where the pieces of this current puzzle go. Unfortunately, this team's shortcomings on the back end are not going away anytime soon, which will make winning enough games to stay in the playoff picture for the remainder of the season a rather difficult task.

By the sounds of it, Oscar Klefbom will be out of action longer than expected, as he is apparently now battling both upper and lower body injuries.

Connor McDavid takes part in practice in Edmonton on January 6, 2016, a little over two months after injuring his collarbone in a game against Philadelphia. He had been out of the lineup since and would not return until February.

Is it fair to expect this kid to hit the ground running upon his return and immediately help Taylor Hall and Leon Draisaitl carry this offence?

Not surprisingly, the Oilers have gone 2–7 since the talented Swede was forced out of the lineup, and chances of that trend changing with the current blue line are not very good. A potential top-six made up of Brandon Davidson, Mark Fayne, Brad Hunt, Eric Gryba, Darnell Nurse, Justin Schultz, and Andrej Sekera is not exactly a comforting thought.

Sorry, but anyone who believes that group is strong enough to allow Edmonton the opportunity to win games with any kind of regularity is either completely off their rocker or simply trying to make the best of a difficult situation. There is little doubt Chiarelli would love nothing more than to upgrade his defence in the here and now, but expecting him to get that done is simply unrealistic. Unless you haven't been paying attention, those are the types of deals that almost never get done during the season in today's NHL.

Make no mistake, having McDavid back in the lineup will undoubtedly give this group a much-needed boost, but even that will wear off at some point. Also, let's not forget that he had played a grand total of 13 games and was just starting to find his legs before getting hurt. The momentum he had gained is all but gone, and one would think there could very well be some signs of hesitation in his game upon returning to the lineup.

The fact McDavid suffered a broken collarbone as opposed to a shoulder injury is likely far better for his long-term health, but the uncertainty a player feels upon returning from a major injury is quite real and rather understandable. With that being the case, is it fair to expect this kid to hit the ground running upon his return and immediately help Taylor Hall and Leon Draisaitl carry this offence?

In my mind, it is not, and that is something that simply cannot be overlooked. We are talking about a player who is roughly two weeks shy of his 19th birthday, and yet he is being looked upon to be some sort of saviour for this team over the next three-and-a-half months. Are we really that delusional? One would hope not, but years upon years of watching losing hockey does odd things to some people.

There is no questioning just how good a player Connor McDavid is and will be over the course of his NHL career, but let's not be silly here. No one player, no matter how talented he is, can fix what is wrong the Edmonton Oilers. That can only be accomplished via trade, drafting, development, and the free-agent market. As of this moment, that job belongs to Peter Chiarelli, and it will be up to him to ensure he surrounds his star attraction with the necessary pieces to help him try and hold up his end of the bargain. ■

This article was adapted from a piece that originally appeared at The Hockey Writers (copyright © January 1, 2016) and is used with permission.

McDavid skating in practice on January 6, 2016.

The Connor and Sid Show

On an evening when Edmonton Oilers centre Connor McDavid made his long-awaited return to the lineup, it seemed fitting that the rookie phenom and Pittsburgh Penguins captain Sidney Crosby were front and centre in Tuesday night's NHL schedule. While the kid wearing No. 97 had an immediate impact in his first game back since breaking his collarbone against the Philadelphia Flyers in early November, No. 87 looked pretty good putting together his most productive performance of the season, picking up his ninth career hat trick.

It is funny how things sometimes tend to play out in the world of sport. From the moment he was selected first overall by the Pens in 2005, Crosby has been viewed as the best player in the game and a generational talent. Sound familiar? Well, it should, because those are the same expectations that have been placed upon McDavid, and most experts tend to believe he will have an even greater impact on the history books when all is said and done.

While we may be just 14 games into his career, it does look as though the youngster is the real deal. The sample size is rather small, but McDavid is already showing signs of being able to dominate, and he just turned 19 years old. He has already shown the knack for doing the improbable at a moment's notice and continued down that path on February 2, 2016, against the Columbus Blue Jackets.

"I think the last time I went on a one-on-two, it didn't end very well for me," said McDavid. "It was a little bit of a better result for me this time. It was a nice goal, I guess. It was three months of waiting around and a lot of grumpy days and all that. It definitely felt really good to get that one." And Oilers fans wasted little time in showing their appreciation in having their star player back in the fold, breaking into a "Connor, Connor" chant in the dying minutes of last night's 5–1 win.

As if delivering a "goal of the year" candidate and putting up a three-point effort in his first game back wasn't already enough, it is the little things that stand out above everything else when it comes to McDavid. Yes, his ability to do things at a ridiculous speed is simply jaw-dropping, but it is the kid's determination to make plays and attempt to get control of every single puck within his reach that is so impressive.

"He set the tone for our team, and our team just followed," said head coach Todd McLellan. "That was as good a first period as we've had all year. I was truly concerned about our ability to jump on them, but we had a good start. Unfortunately, we were down after the first, but he was the catalyst from the drop of the puck."

Be it on the forecheck, in the neutral zone, or his own end of the rink, McDavid seemingly never stops pursuing, and it is both frightening and a joy to watch. Few players in today's game seem as determined as this kid, and with his skillset, who knows where this goes?

Top: A fan holds up a sign welcoming back Edmonton Oilers center Connor McDavid after his return from injury at Rexall Place. *Bottom*: McDavid skates during warm-ups before taking on the Columbus Blue Jackets on February 2, 2016, in his first game since breaking his collarbone in a game on November 3, 2015.

McDavid scores against Blue Jackets goalie Joonas Korpisalo in the second period of his first game back from injury after three months.

"I think what really helped was my opening shift," said McDavid. "I was obviously feeling a bit nervous, but to get the puck that many times on an opening shift, it helps to get a little bit of confidence back and feel good. I didn't expect to be able to do that or play that kind of game. I was happy with how I felt. My timing and all that felt pretty good. It was one game, and I have a bunch left."

While the passing of the torch could happen much sooner than many had anticipated, expecting Crosby to willingly relinquish his crown would be a mistake. After struggling for much of the first half of the season to find his game, the two-time Art Ross Trophy winner has been on an absolute tear of late and managed to light the Ottawa Senators up for three goals and a season-high four points on Tuesday night.

"I think it's fun to play in a wide-open game," said Crosby. "You don't play in that many of them. You have to embrace it. It's one of those games where you know everything's bouncing wacky out there and you want to be on the right side of it. So, if you're complaining, or if you're not happy with the way it's going, you're more likely not to embrace it. I just think you try to make sure you get the last one."

Since the start of the New Year, no player in the league has scored more goals (11) than the 28-year-old pivot, and he appears to be getting better with each and every game. In the blink of an eye, Crosby has gone from being completely out of the picture in the scoring race to suddenly finding himself at No. 14 on the list with 20 goals and 45 points, and is another hot stretch away from cracking the top five.

Not too shabby for a guy who many felt may be hitting a bit of a wall in what has truly been a wonderful career, despite dealing with severe concussion issues that likely cost him what would have been some of his most productive seasons. Going back in time and changing that is not an option, but Crosby still has plenty of gas left in the tank.

In a perfect world, it would be fantastic for hockey fans everywhere to have the privilege of watching both Sidney Crosby and Connor McDavid perform at an elite level for the foreseeable future. Again, at some point, we will see the transition occur from No. 87 to No. 97 as the premier player in the game, but one can only hope that McDavid's drive to be the best will help push Crosby to be even better in the coming years. ■

This article was adapted from a piece that originally appeared at The Hockey Writers (copyright © February 3, 2016) and is used with permission.

Above: The Pittsburgh Penguins' Sidney Crosby (87) celebrates with teammate Patric Hornqvist (72) after completing a hat trick in a game against the Ottawa Senators in Pittsburgh. *Opposite*: On the same night, February 2, 2016, McDavid celebrates his goal against Columbus in the second period. McDavid scored three points on a goal and two assists in the Oilers' 5–1 win.

Flair for the Dramatic

So much for working his way back into things slowly. Since returning from a three-month hiatus courtesy of a broken collarbone, Connor McDavid wasted little time in putting a stamp on his return to the lineup. While the start to his rookie campaign may not have gone as most had envisioned, his second kick at the can has been a resounding success. After creating a buzz throughout the hockey world after a breathtaking effort against the Columbus Blue Jackets, the kid didn't miss a step since rejoining his teammates.

With seven points in five games and playing his best hockey of the season, McDavid looked to be getting better with every shift he took. Call it a stroke of genius by the schedule makers or just dumb luck on the part of the league, but Edmonton had none other than the struggling Toronto Maple Leafs up next on their dance card. That's right, the team many believed to be the landing spot No. 97 was hoping for on the night of the 2015 Draft Lottery was coming to town with the youngster clicking on all cylinders.

After being forced to miss his chance at playing at the Air Canada Centre in late November, a 3–0 victory for the home side, it would only be natural for McDavid to have circled this one on his calendar. With a trip to Toronto no longer part of the equation in 2015–16, this would be his one and only opportunity to put together a performance to remember against the organization he cheered for as a child. Wayne Gretzky was in the same boat throughout his career and made a point of playing some of his best hockey, be it as an Oiler or member of the Los Angeles Kings, against the Maple Leafs.

Not surprisingly, No. 99 did it with a flair for the dramatic on more than a few occasions, and chances are the new kid on the block was hoping for similar success. "I'm looking forward to it," said McDavid. "It was obviously my team growing up, growing up in and around Toronto. They were the sports team I followed the most, and it's going to be really cool to get a chance to play against them." In other words, be prepared as this could turn out to be one of those nights.

With the Maple Leafs dressing a top line of Michael Grabner, Peter Holland, and Leo Komarov, the opportunity was simply too good for the young phenom to allow to slip through his fingers. When all was said and done, the line of McDavid, Jordan Eberle, and Benoit Pouliot had themselves a night to remember in what was a 5–2 Oilers victory and special moment for the kid from Richmond Hill.

Eberle notched his first career hat trick and finished the evening with four points. Pouliot chipped in with four assists of his own, but McDavid topped them all with the first five-point (2 goals, 3 assists) effort of his career. As expected, the magnitude of the moment was not lost on the youngster, and like Gretzky before him, doing it against this opponent made it all the more memorable.

Connor McDavid battles for the puck with the Toronto Maple Leafs' Morgan Rielly in the first period of the Oilers' 5–2 victory over the rookie's hometown team on February 11, 2016, in Edmonton.

McDavid skates past the Maple Leafs' Leo Komarov on his way to the first five-point game of his NHL career.

"It's pretty special, looking across and seeing that logo during warm-up kind of gave me the chills," said McDavid. "So it was special to have a game like that against them. We needed this." It certainly was, and the Oilers definitely did, after dropping three straight to close out a rather disappointing four-game trek out east. To their credit, Toronto was far from terrible on the night but was simply incapable of containing Edmonton's top line.

"You just watch the stuff he can do, the little things most players don't see," Leafs defenceman Jake Gardiner said. "He was in on all five goals tonight. He is definitely a guy you'll have to be aware of. He's right up there with the best players in the league. Such a young guy, to be this good is surprising, for sure. I've heard a lot of things about him, but actually seeing him play, he's pretty good."

As impressive as his performance was, it was the Oilers' bench boss who summed up the evening's proceedings best. "What can you say about Connor?" Todd McLellan said. "His performance did all of the speaking. You watch him and turn into a fan as coaches and players." As do we all. The great thing about McDavid is night in and night out he does something that brings us out of our seats as fans of the game.

McDavid scores one of his two goals against Toronto Maple Leafs goalie Jonathan Bernier.

Do fans of the Oilers take greater pleasure in watching him do his thing than most? Of course, they do, but when you see this kid go on one jaw-dropping rush after another and another and another, it becomes next to impossible to not marvel at what we are watching. And the best part of all is he looks to be having a blast doing it—as any teenager likely would.

The opening goal of last night's tilt with the Leafs was a perfect example. A darting dash, sublime finish, fist-pump celebration and instant eruption of Rexall Place. This kind of thing has happened with such frequency that it is has already started to become an expectation from most inside the building, and the kid is all of 19 games into his career. Do you realize how absurd that sounds?

But that is what the best of the best bring to the table. No matter the sport, there are those handful of elite athletes who have something that sets them apart from all the rest. Some of us have been lucky enough to experience at various times in the past, whereas others are soaking it in for the first time and are simply awestruck by what they are watching. My advice to those people is quite simple: get used to it, folks, because when it comes to Connor McDavid, the best is still to come. ◼

McDavid celebrates after scoring against Toronto.

McDavid vs. Eichel

As much as the NHL would love to see a rivalry form between Connor McDavid and Jack Eichel over the next decade, there is an extremely good chance that nothing of the sort will ever materialize. Contrary to popular belief, the reason hockey fans will not be treated to another Sidney Crosby vs. Alexander Ovechkin–styled showdown over the foreseeable future has nothing to do with the fact the Buffalo Sabres and Edmonton Oilers play in different conferences and everything to do with how good a player No. 97 is going to be.

While it only seemed natural for these two can't-miss prospects to be hyped as the league's next great one-two punch heading into the 2015 Entry Draft, there really is nothing to it. As good a player as the Sabres' young rookie appears to be, there is almost zero chance of Eichel ever approaching the level McDavid seems destined to reach. Like it or not, that is the reality of the situation, and that does not make the talented American any less of a player. Again, it only further solidifies just how good McDavid is.

"He's a big-time player and scores big-time goals," Todd McLellan said following the Oilers' 2–1 overtime victory over the Sabres in which McDavid scored the winner. "I think it's a reflection on him when he downplays it. What's important to Connor is the team. He knows he is an important part and going to be an important part moving forward. But he puts the team in front of himself all the time. To have those qualities as a young superstar is exceptional. A lot of them don't get that at an early age and have to learn that as they go."

There is a reason why we seldom hear anyone use the phrase "generational talent" when describing young players heading into their draft year, and that is because they are a very rare breed. The NHL has had the good fortune to have many talented individuals help grow this game to the level it has reached, but in the grand scheme of things, there has really only been a handful of players who deserve to be included on such a list, and you can pretty much guess who they are.

Outside of the legendary Valeri Kharlamov, who was never granted the opportunity to leave the Soviet Union to play in the NHL prior to his untimely death in 1981, hockey has had a grand total of three generational players in the last half a century: Bobby Orr, Wayne Gretzky, and Mario Lemieux. In my opinion, neither Crosby nor Ovechkin belong in that group, though a healthy No. 87 may have had a shot at joining them—but even that would have been a stretch.

The two most important things the trio of Gretzky, Lemieux, and Orr all had in common was their ability to dominate and change how the game was played. No player has done that since the days of "99 and 66," but the Oilers' rookie phenom looks as though he is headed down that very same path. Obviously, comparing him to the greatest players this game has ever seen after a

Connor McDavid faces off against the Buffalo Sabres' rookie center, the No. 2 overall 2015 draft pick Jack Eichel, during the Edmonton Oilers' 2–1 overtime victory on March 1, 2016, in Buffalo, New York.

grand total of 28 games seems absurd, but that is the beauty in all of this.

Simply go and ask anyone who watched those guys do their thing at the height of their powers, and they will all tell you the same thing—McDavid is the real deal. This kid is special. We have already seen flashes of his brilliance, and he just turned 19 years old in mid-January. By season's end, McDavid will have 45 games of NHL experience under his belt, and you would be hard-pressed to find any rational critic or fan who would not consider him an Art Ross Trophy favourite for the 2016–17 season in what will be his sophomore campaign.

While the hype surrounding the showdown between Jack Eichel and Connor McDavid was easily justifiable and rather enjoyable to watch unfold, there is no need to get carried away. This is not currently, nor will it ever be a two-man race to see who ultimately turns out to be the better player. Again, he is in a class of his own, and there is no shame in admitting that. Greatness is what makes sport so special, and we are about to be treated to exactly that over the next decade, so sit back and enjoy the ride, because it could be quite a while before we seen anything like it again. ∎

This article was adapted from a piece that originally appeared at The Hockey Writers (copyright © March 3, 2016) and is used with permission.

Above: Buffalo fans have to be thinking about what could have been as they watch Edmonton's rookie sensation Connor McDavid celebrate his game-winning goal in the Oilers' overtime win over the Sabres. *Opposite*: Oilers teammates mob McDavid after the clinching goal, while Sabres rookie Jack Eichel skates away dejected.

End of Season, World Championships, and NHL Awards

As far as rookie seasons go, one would be hard-pressed to find anything to complain about when it comes to Connor McDavid. Outside of being forced to miss 37 games due to a broken collarbone, there wasn't much that went wrong with his first go-round. Despite playing just 45 games, the talented youngster managed to finish 2015–16 with the third-highest points-per-game average at 1.07, trailing only Patrick Kane and Jamie Benn. In case you hadn't noticed, those happen to be the last two winners of the Art Ross Trophy as the league's top scorer.

Pretty darn impressive for a 19-year-old who was being asked to not only carry the offensive load for the Edmonton Oilers but also become the new face of the franchise, if not the entire NHL. On the surface, it seemed like quite the burden for a kid to have placed on his shoulders, and yet it was one he seemed rather comfortable with. His final totals of 16 goals and 48 points were good enough for him to finish fourth in rookie scoring, trailing only Chicago Blackhawks forward Artemi Panarin (77), Buffalo Sabres centre Jack Eichel (56), and Maxi Domi (52) of the Arizona Coyotes, but we'll get to more on that later.

Unfortunately, the Oilers season did not play out quite so well. After showing signs of life following McDavid's return, Edmonton proceeded to go 9–14–3 after their young superstar torched the Maple Leafs for five points in mid-February. Not surprisingly, those struggles led to the club finishing the year at the bottom of the Western Conference standings. Sound familiar? Well, it should, as the organization has specialized in it for the better part of the past decade. On the bright side, they did win seven more games than the previous season and hit the 70-point mark for just the third time in 10 years.

It may not sound like much, but McDavid's arrival, coupled with the acquisitions of Andrej Sekera and

Edmonton Oilers center Connor McDavid in action during his rookie season in a game against Buffalo in March 2016.

McDavid tries to get a shot past Philadelphia Flyers' goalie Michal Neuvirth during a game in March 2016. Despite only playing in 45 games in his first NHL season due to injury, McDavid still scored 48 points, finishing fourth among all rookies.

Cam Talbot, gives the team key pieces they did not have following the 2014–15 season, and are much better off for it. Make no mistake, Todd McLellan's expectation for his new club did not include them finishing in last place. On the flipside of the equation, challenging for a playoff spot was always a best-case scenario. But the roster simply wasn't good enough, and it showed down the stretch. Not ideal, but certainly not unexpected.

While 16 teams around the league were preparing for the start of the playoffs, the Oilers were one of 14 teams who had players clearing out their lockers and saying good-bye until next fall's training camp. However, that wasn't case for everybody, as seven players were headed to Russia to represent their home countries at the 2016 IIHF World Championship. Leon Draisaitl and Sekera would be playing for Team Germany and Team Slovakia, respectively, while forwards Matt Hendricks and Patrick Maroon would be wearing the Red, White, and Blue of Team USA.

The trio of Taylor Hall, McDavid, and Talbot would not only play for Team Canada, all three were being counted on to be key contributors in helping Canada defend their title from a year ago. Outside of watching their squad drop a meaningless game to Team Finland during the preliminary round, Bill Peters and his staff could not have asked for much more from his club during the two-week event. From start to finish, it was a complete team effort, and all three Oilers players held up their end of the bargain.

Talbot was solid throughout the tournament and pitched a shutout in the finale, helping backstop Canada to a 2–0 victory against Finland in the gold medal game. After struggling to find chemistry with one another in Edmonton during the early stages of the NHL season, Peters decided to give the Hall-McDavid combination another look-see at the Worlds, and the duo did not disappoint. Hall wound up leading Canada in goals with six, and McDavid managed to do the same on the assist front, notching eight over 10 games.

Both saw plenty of ice time against Canada's tougher opponents, and in typical No. 97 fashion, the kid would score his only goal of the tournament in the final—and it was the game-winner. It was unquestionably his best game of the tournament, as he was a threat each and every time he jumped over the boards, and it came when it mattered most. "Before the game, I told him I had a good feeling about him," teammate Mark Scheifele said. "He's an unbelievable player and he was awesome tonight. It just goes to show what type of guy and what type of player he is."

Toronto Maple Leafs blueliner Morgan Rielly echoed a similar sentiment about the NHL Rookie of the Year candidate. "You could tell before the game. He was zoned in and ready to go," Rielly said. "When he comes out and is skating the way he was today, it gives us a real good chance to win." Success on the International stage is nothing new for McDavid, but with Canada's victory in Moscow, the 2015 first overall pick became the youngest player ever to win gold at the World Under-18, World Junior Championship, and World Championship.

With his first pro season now under his belt and some much-needed rest in his immediate future, there was one only one more question left to answer. Would Connor McDavid win the Calder Trophy as the top rookie of 2015–16? Despite missing almost half the season due to injury, he was one of three finalists for the Rookie of the Year along with Panarin and Philadelphia Flyers defenceman Shayne Gostisbehere. As good a year as both those players had, one would be hard-pressed to make a strong argument against either one finishing ahead of the Oilers' new prized possession in the voting.

McDavid scores a goal for Team Canada during the 2016 IIHF World Championship final match against Finland.

McDavid, captain of Team North America for the World Cup of Hockey, celebrates teammate Auston Matthews' goal against Sweden with Mark Scheifele, Morgan Rielly, and Colton Parayko (far right) during a game in Toronto on September 21, 2016.

After all, the trophy is to be awarded "to the player selected as the most proficient in his first year of competition in the National Hockey League." Even though Panarin, who was 24 years of age at season's end, teamed with Patrick Kane to form the league's most productive scoring duo, McDavid was still the better choice. He scored at a higher rate and made those around him better, more so than any other rookie. Ultimately, it would come down to who the Professional Hockey Writers' Association felt deserved the award most, and in the end, they got it wrong.

While not the choice I would have made, with the overall point spread between Panarin and McDavid being what it was, seeing the Blackhawks marksman come out on top was by no means a shock. What was rather perplexing is that Gostisbehere was next in voting. With all due respect to the American rearguard, who was fantastic in helping lead the Flyers to the postseason, it made no sense. The fact there were 80 voters who did not have McDavid first or second on their ballot is staggering. And even more mystifying, there were nine who did not have him inside the top

2015–16 Calder Trophy Voting	Points (1st / 2nd / 3rd / 4th / 5th)
1. Artemi Panarin, CHI	1,258 (88 / 41 / 16 / 3 / 2)
2. Shayne Gostisbehere, PHI	955 (33 / 53 / 42 / 12 / 8)
3. Connor McDavid, EDM	858 (25 / 45 / 48 / 15 / 8)

five. In the grand scheme of things, it is not that big of a deal, but it's the principle of it that looks terrible.

Let's not forget, this is the same guy who was named NHL Rookie of the Month in all three months he played, and yet the voting played out in the fashion it did. "It doesn't matter, I'm just happy to be in Vegas," McDavid said. "It was a good rookie class, so it's good for him. It was just cool to be here and experience this." When asked if he learned any lessons from his first season that could be taken into his sophomore campaign, his answer was rather telling: "Don't go into the boards too hard.…I think that's something I learned…but I'm just excited to get the second season started."

Challenge accepted. ∎

McDavid vs. Matthews Impact

The NHL released its 2016–17 schedule on Tuesday, and while there was never going to be any surprises when it came to match-ups, as it is the same drill each and every year, there was something that stood out as a bit of a head-scratcher. While it may not seem like that big of a deal to fans in the United States, the fact the Edmonton Oilers and Toronto Maple Leafs do not square off on *Hockey Night in Canada* in either one of their two meetings is rather perplexing.

With rumblings starting to make the rounds that Rogers is seriously considering swapping out *HNIC* host George Stroumboulopoulos with his predecessor Ron MacLean, things appear to be on shaky ground. It has become painfully obvious the ratings the network was hoping to gain when they decided to cough up $5.2 billion to acquire the rights to essentially become the sole broadcaster of NHL games across Canada have fallen well short of expectation, and changes are coming.

With that being the case, one would think putting some "must-see-television" over their airwaves would be a priority of sorts. So would it not make perfect sense for the NHL to feature a Connor McDavid–led Oilers side in head-to-head battles against Auston Matthews and the Maple Leafs on a coast-to-coast broadcast on a Saturday evening? Seems pretty cut and dried from here, but that is clearly not the case.

With the two teams playing in different conferences, fans can only be treated to this match-up twice a season, and the powers that be decided to have them play both those games on … wait for it … a pair of Tuesday nights in November. Confused? Well, you should be. And if you answered that question with a no, please let me in on the gag because this makes absolutely no sense from my end of the spectrum. So much for riding that hype-machine for all it's worth.

While it would not surprise me in the least if one or maybe even both of these games end up being part of a mid-week *HNIC* broadcast before all is said and done, my question is why bother even going down that road? You already have the opportunity to use both encounters as a centrepiece of sorts for Rogers, simply schedule it accordingly and go from there. Instead, the NHL decides to do their supposed partner in crime no favours on the scheduling front, and we are left to sit here and wonder why.

It is not as if this is some kind of foreign concept. Toronto has traditionally had games scheduled on Saturday nights for ages, and Edmonton has 15 dates

The Oilers' 2015 No. 1 overall draft pick Connor McDavid faces the Toronto Maple Leafs' 2016 No. 1 overall pick, center Auston Matthews during a break in the first period of the Oilers–Maple Leafs matchup on Tuesday, November 1, 2016, in Toronto.

of their own on the schedule in 2016–17. Obviously, the lack of success of the seven Canadian teams has played a big role in Rogers' rating struggles, but that is something that is out of both their and the league's control. However, that is not the case when it comes to programming, and there is frankly no excuse for this sort of oversight.

While a computer may spit out the NHL schedule on an annual basis, it should not be that difficult to ensure a couple of games are placed on evenings in which they can be used to help drive viewership and ultimately get more eyeballs on the game. Come on, now, does someone really need to let those in charge know that a McDavid vs. Matthews match-up might do okay from a numbers standpoint in this country? At this stage of the game, this sort of thing should be a no-brainer for all parties involved, and yet here we are.

If nothing else, at least use the games to help promote the popular *Hometown Hockey* series that runs on Sportsnet across the country on Sunday evenings over the course of the season but has yet to bring in strong numbers on a consistent basis. It would instantly give them a platform to potentially do something special with the broadcast, and that should be priority one for both the NHL and Rogers. In the grand scheme of things, a couple of games between a pair of bottom feeders may not seem like a big deal, but it certainly is an opportunity missed.

From the moment Edmonton won the 2015 Draft Lottery and had McDavid fall into its lap, fans outside of the Alberta capital have been crying foul, and much of Leafs nation has been driving that bus. In the blink of an eye, Toronto lost the opportunity to add a generational talent for the first time in their storied history, and he was a Maple Leafs fan growing up to

boot. It certainly hit a nerve with much of the fan base, and who could blame them?

To make matters worse, they were not even granted the opportunity of watching the kid do his thing in his own backyard during the 2015–16 campaign, as McDavid was out of action with a broken collarbone during the Oilers' lone visit to Toronto. Add to that the fact he torched the Leafs for a season-high five points in early February over at Rexall Place, and the love-hate relationship only grew further with No. 97.

Fast forward to the present day, and fans in Toronto have clearly moved on and can hardly wait to see Matthews pull on a Blue and White jersey on Friday night after hearing his name called as the first overall pick in the 2016 NHL Entry Draft. While no one is putting the talented American on the same level as McDavid, he has the potential to become a superstar in this league for years to come. Both these kids are expected to lead their respective teams to something special, so why not take advantage of all the hype? Seems logical enough.

Again, when all is said and done, having the Oilers face off against the Maple Leafs on *Hockey Night in Canada* is really not a huge deal. This league has bigger fish to fry, and making their game more exciting to watch is high on that list. With that said, it does seem rather odd that neither the NHL nor Rogers seem overly interested in promoting a head-to-head match-up between two of the best young players in the game, and both happen to play in hockey-crazed Canadian markets. It just doesn't add up, and it makes zero sense. ■

This article was adapted from a piece that originally appeared at The Hockey Writers (copyright © June 22, 2016) and is used with permission.

The Maple Leafs' Leo Komarov (47) and Nikita Zaitsev (22) try to stop McDavid in the second period of the two teams' second meeting, on Tuesday, November 29, 2016, in Edmonton.

Three Scoring Lines

It may be hard to believe, but it appears as though the Edmonton Oilers have three centres capable of playing top-six minutes for the first time in franchise history. While the guys wearing No. 99 and No. 11 drove the bus during the "Glory Years," none of those teams featured the potential three-headed monster Todd McLellan will have at his disposal in 2016–17.

With that said, one can't help but wonder if the presence of Connor McDavid won't ultimately force the Oilers to be a little more creative in their approach.

As intriguing as the notion of watching the trio of Leon Draisaitl, Ryan Nugent-Hopkins, and McDavid might be, there is only so much ice time to go around. Having four units that can contribute to the cause is a necessity in today's game, but giving anything more than 20 minutes of combined time to the third and fourth lines would be a major mistake on a team that has an elite talent waiting in the wings. Sorry, but no matter how you slice it, the math simply doesn't work.

By the sounds of it, the Oilers are hoping to put together a fourth line that could deliver close to 10 minutes of useful hockey on a nightly basis. Going down that road would leave roughly 50 minutes to be divided up between the remaining three lines, and if McDavid isn't getting at least 22 of those, there is an issue. That leaves approximately 28 minutes for Draisaitl and Nugent-Hopkins to share. Are you starting to see the problem?

Nugent-Hopkins has proven to be more than capable of logging in the neighbourhood of 19 to 20 minutes a night and has never had the good fortune of having a running mate like McDavid. Using that approach, Draisaitl would be left with nothing more than scraps in a traditional third-line set-up. However, that can easily be rectified by giving the talented German some gravy time on the wing with the 2015 first overall pick.

As things currently sit, Edmonton has Jordan Eberle, Milan Lucic, Patrick Maroon, Benoit Pouliot, Jesse Puljujarvi, and Nail Yakupov slated to see regular duty inside the Oilers top nine. By the sounds of it, Eberle and Lucic will be given the first crack at playing with McDavid, and history suggests the duo of Nugent-Hopkins and Yakupov are not a good fit.

Meaning two of Maroon, Pouliot, and Puljujarvi will find their way onto a line with Nugent-Hopkins and the other will join Yakupov, if he's still around, on line No. 3. Again, rolling three units is a waste when you have a player like McDavid at your disposal. Someone is going to be forced into giving up some ice, and it certainly should not be the kid wearing No. 29 on his back.

Edmonton's Leon Draisaitl (29), Adam Larsson (center-left), Andrej Sekera (center-right), and Connor McDavid (97) celebrate a goal during a 3–2 overtime victory over the New Jersey Devils on January 12, 2017, in Edmonton, Alberta.

Oilers right wing Jordan Eberle (14) and center Connor McDavid (97) prepare for a faceoff against the Ottawa Senators in October 2016 in Edmonton.

In my mind, splitting Draisaitl's time between centre and the wing could arguably be the best thing for him. Let's not forget he has yet to show the ability to drive a line at this level but did a fantastic job of riding shotgun with Taylor Hall during the first half of 2015–16. Call me crazy, but my guess is most teams would want no part of handing their so-called "soft-minutes" line the job of having to deal with a Draisaitl-McDavid combo over the course of 60 minutes.

From a matchup standpoint, this has disaster written all over it for opposing coaches. If the Oilers were to take said approach, it truly would be a "pick your poison" scenario for teams and force them to make a choice and hope for the best. However, if Edmonton decides to run with the traditional top-nine set-up, that would not be the case.

Obviously, this puts a heavier workload on McDavid, but something tells me this kid wants that extra load on his shoulders. It may seem like a lot to put on a 19-year-old in his second season in the NHL, but everyone needs to accept this isn't your everyday, run-of-the-mill player. Take a look at last year's league leaders in time-on-ice among forwards, and you'll see there was not one player who averaged 22 minutes a night during the 2015–16 season.

There were two players who were north of 21 minutes, and both happened to play for the Buffalo Sabres in Ryan O'Reilly (21:44) and Evander Kane (21:02). In fact, only 12 forwards in the entire league averaged at least 20 minutes of ice a night, and most of the names on that list are rather predictable. However, none of the players listed—Sidney Crosby and Alexander Ovechkin included—are in the same stratosphere as McDavid.

In the eyes of some, that may be a bit of a stretch, but my eyes tell me we are about to watch something special unfold over the next few years. The NHL has not seen a player like this since the days of Wayne Gretzky and Mario Lemieux. They are a rare breed, and if an organization is fortunate enough to have one fall into its lap, they have little choice but to loosen the reins and let him go.

While the game is far different today than it was during the 1980s, it was not uncommon to see Gretzky and Mark Messier take on 45 minutes of ice-time between them on a nightly basis. Not surprisingly, the NHL's all-time scoring leader was regularly double-shifted and used in all situations. No. 99 not only saw a ridiculous amount of time on the man advantage, but was also a regular fixture on one of the Oilers' penalty killing units.

You can bet the Richmond Hill native will start receiving similar treatment during his sophomore campaign. It may be a different era, but getting your best players on the ice as much as possible remains a priority for any head coach, and McLellan is no different. Now, will there be evenings when this is not the case? Most certainly, but let's not kid ourselves here.

As of this moment, the only player on this roster who has shown the ability to be a driver at this level is McDavid, and this staff will make sure he is used appropriately. Again, putting together three scoring lines may be what fans want to see, and one can understand why.

Yet the chances of that coming to fruition appear rather slim, and there is nothing wrong with that. This roster doesn't have the necessary horses to put together three scoring lines but certainly does have enough fire-power for Connor McDavid and company to carry the load up front, and the Edmonton Oilers should be better off for it. ■

This article was adapted from a piece that originally appeared at The Hockey Writers (copyright © August 7, 2016) and is used with permission.

Oilers left wing Patrick Maroon (19) celebrates his goal against the Bruins with teammates Connor McDavid (97), Leon Draisaitl (29), and Oscar Klefbom (77) during a game on January 5, 2017, in Boston.

Dawning of a New Era

As far as individual team honours go, there is arguably nothing most hockey players take greater pride in than being made part of a leadership group inside the dressing room. It may only be a letter on a sweater to some, but to others it actually holds meaning. It is something rarely placed onto the shoulders of young players in the NHL, let alone those who are still teenagers. However, when it comes to Connor McDavid, the norm is almost never part of the equation.

After leading Team North America to what turned out to be a memorable showing at the 2016 World Cup, the 19-year-old was handed quite the honour shortly after arriving at training camp. In what was one of the worst-kept secrets in hockey, the Edmonton Oilers officially unveiled McDavid as the 15th captain in franchise history on October 5, making him the youngest captain in league history.

"I'm very honoured and humbled to be able to wear the C for this organization," McDavid said. "There are so many good leaders in this room, and to be able to represent them is definitely a good feeling."

When asked whether he felt overwhelmed by the news, the answer given was one that we would typically hear from a tenured veteran, not a kid about to enter his sophomore campaign. "No, it doesn't feel overwhelming at all … I just feel normal about it. I'm very humbled to wear it and excited about it," McDavid said. "But having the support of my teammates and all that is the main thing, and that's what makes it so much easier. I think I'm a guy who can relate to everyone and is very close with everyone on the team. I try and bring guys together and all that. I think that's what I tried to focus on in Erie, and it felt like everyone was a part of a team. I definitely try and lead that way… I'm not the big 'rah-rah' kind of guy."

Again, not exactly the kind of response you expect to hear from someone with a grand total of 45 games under his belt. Even more remarkable was the way in which the message was delivered. There were no wide-eyed, in-over-his-head looks or sheepish, ear-to-ear grins. In fact, it was the complete opposite. The reaction was more one of acceptance that comes with the added responsibility of the role and not one of sheer happiness.

Let's not forget, the first overall selection in the 2015 Entry Draft didn't pull any punches when asked by TSN's Hockey Insider Darren Dreger on the possibility of becoming the club's next captain during the 2016 IIHF World Championship. "I'm looking to have a good summer, come into training camp, and whether or not it happens, that's a different story," said

The Edmonton Oilers' new captain, Connor McDavid, skates during warmups prior to an NHL preseason game against the Winnipeg Jets on October 6, 2016, at Rogers Place.

McDavid. "I want to come to camp and show everyone that I'm not some young 19-year-old anymore, and I'm ready to take a bigger role."

Contrary to what some in the national media were suggesting at the time, the Oilers did not rush or err in making the decision they did. By the end of his rookie season, it became abundantly clear to anyone who was paying attention that this had become No. 97's team. Even those who were lukewarm to the idea had little choice but to come around after hearing his head coach and teammates speak in such glowing terms about the kid…and it was genuine.

"He is mature beyond his years," Todd McLellan said. "He's dealt with all of you since he was 14. He handles himself very well and takes care of his teammates in front of and with the media, which we think is very important for a Canadian franchise. He is an ambassador of the game, which I think you have to be as a captain. He puts himself out there with the fans and the young kids, and he understands his role. Sidney Crosby and a couple of others have gone through that, they do a tremendous job, and I see a lot of that in him."

"I think the writing was on the wall there," said netminder Cam Talbot. "There is no better guy to lead this team than one of the most exciting and best players in the league. I don't think they could have chosen a better guy for the job."

Even to a player like Milan Lucic, who was new to the party and partially brought on board to assist with changing the so-called culture inside the dressing room, the decision seemed rather obvious. "There is no better person to lead this team forward," Lucic said. "And it is my job and everyone else's to make sure we follow his lead."

"For everyone in the room, he's a great example of how you go out there and play every night," said Darnell Nurse. "He takes it to a new level and definitely

McDavid during training camp in September 2016.

brings energy every night that we can feed off of. For a leader, for a captain, you want to follow a good example, and there's no better example than a guy who comes in every day, takes care of what he puts into his body, and does everything he can in the gym and on the ice. The captain really leads first by example, and he's a textbook example of that."

No matter where you turned, the praises for McDavid continued to roll in, but perhaps the most telling of all came courtesy of the team's elder statesman. "He is not just a special player…he is going to be a special team leader," said veteran winger Matt Hendricks. "He has a unique swagger in that he is confident in his ability, but he never puts himself ahead of the team." And that is it in a nutshell. We are not talking about some run-of-the-mill player here, and that changes everything.

With all due respect to Colorado Avalanche forward Gabriel Landeskog, who was the youngest captain in league history prior to McDavid, no one has taken on the role with this much fanfare since Crosby in 2007. Both were looked upon as saviours for long-suffering franchises that, ironically enough, enjoyed years of success with the last two generational talents to make their way to the NHL. It's not every day that players are expected to try and live up to the standards of Wayne Gretzky and Mario Lemieux.

The difference being that Crosby had two full seasons and a scoring title to his credit before having the C placed on his sweater. With Edmonton's current struggles and roster construction being what they are, giving McDavid another year to get comfortable in his NHL skin wasn't an option, and the kid wanted it. Safe to say, it will likely be a decision that neither the player nor organization will regret. ■

McDavid calls the play during the NHL Heritage Classic against the Jets in Winnipeg on October 23, 2016. McDavid became the youngest captain in NHL history in early October at the age of 19.

Turning the Page

In hockey, eight years is an awfully long time. That is the amount of time that elapsed from the moment Daryl Katz officially took over ownership of the Edmonton Oilers in the summer of 2008, to the opening of Rogers Place in the fall of 2016. While the team was among the worst in all of hockey during said stretch, posting a dreadful 225–320–77 record, the continual off-ice hurdles surrounding the project were arguably even more painful to live through.

It may have taken longer than anyone had envisioned, but in the end the city of Edmonton and Mr. Katz worked together in delivering the world-class, multipurpose arena that was promised all those years ago. With the building finally in place, the focus could now shift back toward trying to restore the winning tradition of one the league's most storied franchises. Fittingly enough, that journey was set to begin on October 12, 2016, against the Calgary Flames to help kick off the 100th season of operation for the National Hockey League.

With the eyes of the hockey world squarely on Rogers Place and what the new-look Oilers would look like to start the year, everyone was hoping for Connor McDavid to christen his new home in spectacular fashion. On a night that started with a look back to the past, as both Wayne Gretzky and Mark Messier took part in the pregame ceremonies, it was an evening in which you got the sense this franchise needed to finally turn the page on its past—both good and bad.

As difficult as the last decade has been for fans and the organization to stomach, the constant reminder of just how special the great Oilers teams of yesteryear were was something few have felt comfortable with. Embracing history is a fantastic thing, but when the past 10 years consisted of nothing but one disastrous campaign after another, a cleaning of the slate was in order to move forward. One couldn't have asked for a better setting to do exactly that, and No. 97 was happy to oblige.

What turned out to eventually be a 7–4 win for the home side was made all the more special by what McDavid did in the span of just over two minutes during the second period. After breaking a 3–3 tie with his first goal of the season midway through the frame, the Richmond Hill native would send Rogers Place into an absolute frenzy 136 seconds later. After being hacked on a clear-cut breakaway by Flames defenceman Dennis Wideman, the young phenom was awarded a penalty shot, and the Oilers' new home was suddenly bubbling over with anticipation.

On the surface, it may not seem like much, but for this fan base and these players, it was a moment in which things could have gone differently. Edmonton had already blown a two-goal lead in typical Oilers

Top left: Edmonton Oilers owner Dave Katz shows off murals on the side of Rogers Place, the newly opened home of the Oilers on October 12, 2016. *Top right*: Wayne Gretzky during opening ceremonies at Rogers Palace. *Bottom*: Edmonton Oilers alumni (from left) Glen Anderson, Jari Kurri, Wayne Gretzky, Mark Messier, Paul Coffey, and Grant Fuhr attend the unveiling of the Wayne Gretzky statue and Hall of Fame room at Rogers Place.

Edmonton Oilers captain Connor McDavid takes a shot on goal during the 2016–17 season opener on October 12 at Rogers Place. McDavid netted two goals and an assist in the Oilers' 7–4 victory.

"You need that type of night from your captain... For a 19-year-old to settle you down like that is remarkable." —Todd McLellan

fashion, courtesy of not one but two short-handed goals. McDavid would have none of it. He stopped them dead in their tracks, scoring all of 86 seconds after Michael Frolik had got Calgary back on level terms. And now he had the opportunity to put a dagger in their heart.

With all of Oilers nation, not to mention the 18,347 in attendance, on the edge of their seats and just waiting to let loose, McDavid delivered in breathtaking fashion. As if the goal weren't already enough to send the masses into in all-out frenzy, the speed and ease with which he was stickhandling the puck as he came in on Brian Elliott seemed almost unfair. Just like that, a tie game turned back into a two-goal cushion for the Oilers, and their new barn had its first genuine eruption.

"He was tremendous tonight," said head coach Todd McLellan. "You need that type of night from your captain, especially when you're putting up a new building where there is some excitement and a few jitters. For a 19-year-old to settle you down like that is remarkable. Credit to him and the followers for following him." It was impressive to watch unfold, and you could feel the sense of relief inside the building—from fans and players alike.

"The anticipation for this game was huge, and the fans were excited with all the greats that were in the building," McDavid said. "It was an exciting night for our whole organization, and it was a good way to start it. I'm kind of happy it's over. I'll definitely take a lot of good memories from tonight and move on with those.

But it's over and now we can get back to our day-to-day routine." Whether because the pressure of the moment was no longer on their shoulders or the friendly schedule in the month of October, the Oilers used the win to help propel them to their best start in ages.

As if the Flames hadn't already had their fill of McDavid in the curtain raiser, he matched his performance in the opener with another three-point effort in the back half of the two sides' home-and-home set to start the year, another Oilers victory. In fact, Edmonton managed to reel off wins against the Carolina Hurricanes, St. Louis Blues, Winnipeg Jets, Washington Capitals, and Vancouver Canucks before the month was out. Good enough for the top spot in the Pacific Division with a 7–2 record.

Not surprisingly, McDavid led the league in scoring with five goals, seven assists, and 12 points, but this was about more than individual point totals. Game in and game out, the kid has had opposing teams on their heels, and they had yet to figure out a way to slow him down in a legal manner. His footspeed was simply too much for teams to handle, and it has led to countless odd-man rushes and breakaways for the talented youngster.

The scary thing is, McDavid was still adjusting to life with new linemates, most notably Milan Lucic, and yet he still produced at the clip he did. Add to that the fact McLellan was smart enough to use his captain in all situations, double shifting him when the opportunity presented itself, and you have a player who was fully engaged from the drop of the puck to the final buzzer. ■

McDavid celebrates one of his two goals against the Calgary Flames during the Oilers' season-opening win.

Round One: McDavid vs. Crosby

It was the head-to-head match-up hockey fans everywhere were dying to see heading into the 2015–16 NHL season. Unfortunately, three days prior to the Connor McDavid vs. Sidney Crosby showdown, the 2015 first overall pick broke his collarbone against the Philadelphia Flyers. As if the injury weren't already enough of a punch to the gut for the game itself, having it happen just days prior to the pair's first meeting, made the entire situation that much harder to stomach.

Disappointing, for sure, but it was just a matter of time before fans would get their wish. Once the 2016–17 schedule was officially released, there was once again a day everyone could circle on their calendars: November 8 in Pittsburgh. Ironically, this time around it was the health of Crosby that could have potentially derailed things, after he started the season on the sideline with concussion-like symptoms. Could disaster strike a second consecutive season?

Thankfully, the 29-year-old would return to the Penguins lineup on October 25 against the Florida Panthers and wasted little time in making his presence felt. With eight goals and 10 points in six games, it was clear Crosby was not only over his concussion but looked to be in mid-season form heading into

their matchup with the Oilers. At the other end of the spectrum, McDavid had started to slow down after a torrid start to his sophomore campaign.

After being named the NHL's First Star of the Month for October, the 19-year-old had only a pair of assists from his last five games and was held off the scoresheet in three of them. Not surprisingly, Edmonton went just 2–2–1 during that stretch, after winning seven of eight to start their year. Let's not forget, McDavid was on a pace for 123 points two weeks into the season, so a regression was bound to occur. With that said, going up against No. 87 is an entirely different ball of wax.

"Tonight is going to be cool for me to play against Crosby, against someone I grew up idolizing and someone I have followed along his career," said McDavid. "I'm definitely excited about that." Make no mistake, the kid was well aware of the expectations on him, and they likely fall short of the ones he places on himself. As cool as facing Crosby would be, it was a measuring stick game of sorts and one that guys like this rarely have the opportunity to play in.

On the flipside of the equation, it's not every day that a guy with the kind of résumé Crosby has gets pushed from what is essentially a first-year player in the

Connor McDavid competes for the puck against the Pittsburgh Penguins' Sidney Crosby in the first period of their first head-to-head matchup on November 8, 2016.

McDavid skates with the puck against the defending Stanley Cup champion Penguins in Pittsburgh, a game the Oilers would lose 4–3, despite McDavid's three assists.

league. "I think once you get out there, that's the best part…the competitive side kind of takes over," said Crosby. "Obviously it will be one that's talked about a little bit more, but at the end of the day, you're going out there, trying to get two points. They all mean the same, but you definitely understand the situation. I think that competition is why you play, that's what you love about the game."

In other words, bring all you got, kid, because I have no intention of relinquishing my crown anytime soon. Does it get any better than this? The heir-apparent was already pushing the boundaries of what the future might hold, despite having played less than a full season's worth of games at the NHL level. Whereas the current king of the mountain is arguably coming off the finest run of his career and looks to be showing no signs of slowing down anytime soon. Some pretty special stuff indeed.

Bringing us to the obvious question: would the duo be able to deliver on the hype? Don't kid yourselves, there is a big difference between doing it when it matters most, opposed to game No. 14 on an 82-game schedule. One is nothing like the other, especially for a player of Crosby's stature. Remember, we are talking about a guy who already has multiple Art Ross and Hart Trophies, as well as a Conn Smythe in his back pocket. Not to mention a pair of Stanley Cup championships and Olympic gold medals.

So while the recognition of the moment was real, there was no guarantee the response would match it. Luckily for all of us, that was not the case when it came to the young phenom. On a night when the defending champs came back from a two-goal deficit to earn a thrilling 4–3 victory, there was no question who the star of the show was. With assists on all three of Edmonton's goals and one breathtaking rush after another, McDavid surely held up his end of the bargain.

The Penguins' Crosby (87) gets off a pass in front of McDavid in the second period of Pittsburgh's 4–3 victory.

McDavid takes the puck out of the Oilers' end, with the Penguins' star center Crosby looking on.

"You can tell that [McDavid] really needs no time and space at all." —Sidney Crosby

The two played head-to-head for much of the evening, and while Crosby was held off the scoresheet for the first time since returning from injury (though he did play crucial roles in two of the Pens' four goals), the kid seized the moment to show what he could do. "It was a good chance for me to kind of measure myself against the best player in the world," said McDavid. "Going head-to-head with him all night was a good test." And one that he passed with flying colours.

"With his speed, he doesn't need a lot of time and space," said Crosby. "It's one thing to kind of watch games and see it, but out there you can tell that he really needs no time and space at all. If you're even with him you're in big trouble, so you'd better make sure you're a step ahead." Hearing that kind of praise from any of your peers has to be an extremely gratifying moment for any player, but to have it come from the mouth of the best player in the world is awfully telling.

Above all else, it is the speed at which McDavid does things that continues to amaze. For example, to have the ability to track down and strip the puck away, in open ice no less, from a skater as renowned as the Penguins' Carl Hagelin is one thing. But to then instantly turn that play into an odd-man rush in the other direction, in which he makes defenceman Brian Dumoulin look like a turnstile, is something we just do not see at this level.

What makes it all the more special is that, after doing all that, this kid possesses the skill-set to throw the kind of touch pass he did to Patrick Maroon, who promptly deposited it in a yawning cage. It almost seems unfair and prompts one to think back to the ever-popular men-against-boys analogy that so many love to use in the sporting world. The problem being, in this case, it is the so-called boy who is schooling the rest, and no one seems to be overly surprised by it—including his head coach.

"I thought his line had the better of that line during the first half of the game," said McLellan. "Connor played very well. There's no other way of putting it, he had a tremendous game. He was effective all over the rink, and that's great. It just goes to show, when you're playing what's likely the best team in the National Hockey League, you need everybody going. It doesn't matter how well the star players play." With all due respect to the Oilers' bench boss, the disappointment with the result was understandable but nothing more than a side story on this night.

Hockey is no different than most team sports. The chances of a team enjoying success are next to impossible without enough quality pieces in place to help carry the load. However, it is different than most in that, every once and while, it gives us the opportunity to see elite talents go *mano a mano*, and when it all comes together, it is exhilarating to watch and something that should not be missed.

With a 10-year difference in age between them and playing in different conferences, a McDavid vs. Crosby match-up is not something we will be treated to as often as any of us would like in the coming years. So when they do pop up on the schedule, my advice to hockey fans everywhere is quite simple: take a step back and simply enjoy the magic while we still can. ■

82-Game Look-In

As the end of the 2016 calender drew to close, Connor McDavid reached a milestone of sorts. After missing nearly half his rookie campaign due to injury, the 2015 first overall pick didn't manage to reach the 82-game mark of his career until December 29, 2016, against the Los Angeles Kings. While combining totals from two different seasons into one is by no means an exact translation as to what a player would have produced from October to April, in this case it seems to paint a fairly accurate picture.

After being held off the scoresheet in the Oilers' 3–1 win over the Kings, McDavid wrapped up his unofficial first year in the NHL with 29 goals, 61 assists, and 90 points. In comparison, both Alex Ovechkin (106) and Sidney Crosby (102) eclipsed the century mark in their rookie seasons. The big difference between the two is, in 2005–06, the league had seven players hit the 100-point plateau and seven more reach the 90-point mark.

In contrast, Patrick Kane (106) was the only player in the game to go over either one of those marks in 2015–16. Need a little more perspective? Not a problem. Over the last three seasons, the NHL has had a grand total of two players, Kane last season and Crosby (104) in 2013–14, post campaigns of 90 points or better. In other words, we are talking apples to oranges here. And when you consider the hurdles

McDavid has had to overcome over the last year and a bit, it makes his performance all the more remarkable.

You name it, and this kid has dealt with it over the past 18 months. First and foremost was the broken collarbone that derailed his rookie season for three months, just as he was starting to feel comfortable in his new surroundings. Second, as if the pressure that comes with being tagged the game's next generational talent weren't already enough, having to deal with it in No. 99's old stomping grounds could not have been easy. How about carrying the weight that comes with being named the youngest captain in league history in a hockey-crazed market?

Add to that a team that was built to revolve around him from the moment he was drafted, and suddenly that 90-point total looks all the more impressive. After averaging 1.07 points per game in 2015–16, McDavid has scored at an even better clip (1.13) through the first two-and-half months of his sophomore season and done it with little help from his regular linemates. Jordan Eberle is in the midst of the worst goal-scoring slump of his career, having lit in the lamp in just six of the Oilers' 37 games, and Milan Lucic has been nowhere near the fit the organization had hoped he would be on the left side.

Contrary to popular belief, finding regular linemates for a generational-type talent is not the easiest thing to do. Peter Chiarelli went out and threw

Connor McDavid is chased by the Sharks' Mikkel Boedker (89) during a game on December 23, 2016, in San Jose, California. McDavid reached 90 points for his career in the game with his 13th goal of the season and an assist.

McDavid celebrates his game-clinching goal during a shootout against the Tampa Bay Lightning in Edmonton on December 17, 2016. The Oilers won 3–2.

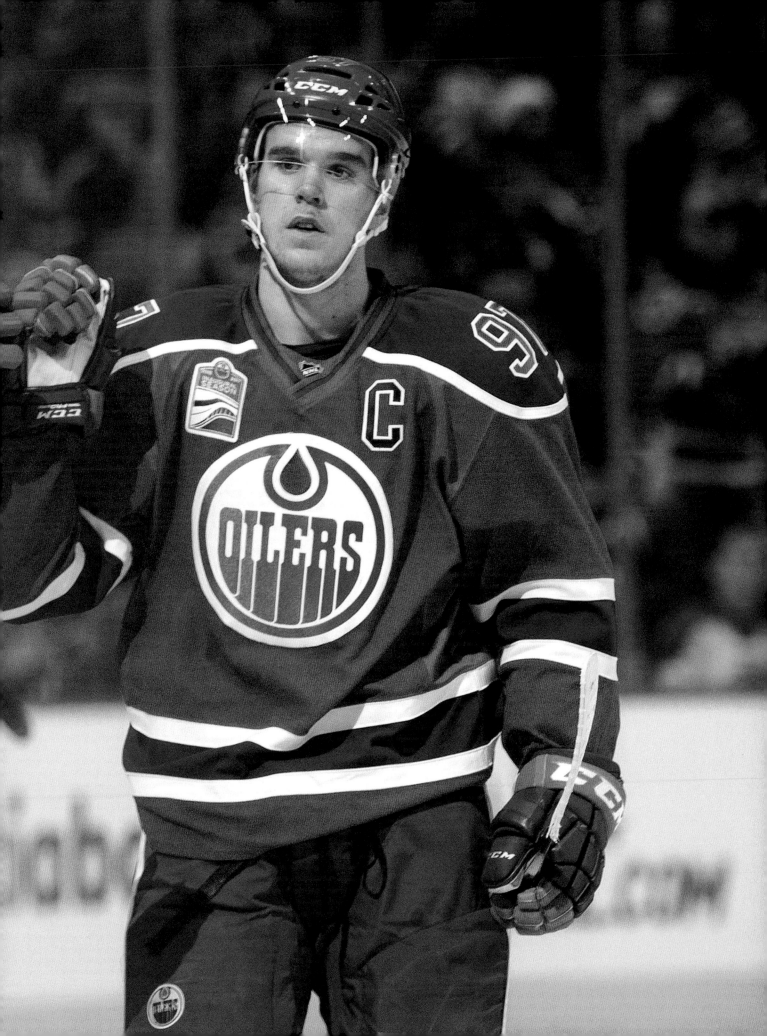

"Three pretty lucky goals…It's a funny league that way. You get Grade A chances, and they're not going in, then you start putting it there and they are going in." —Connor McDavid

$42 million over the next seven years at Lucic via unrestricted free agency, hoping he had acquired the perfect piece to use with the game's next great talent. Unfortunately, it was a combination that has yet to pay off, and there is a good chance it never will. While the notion of having the hulking winger run shotgun with McDavid was all well and good, his limitations as a player and inability to process the game at the same level as No. 97 is problematic and not likely to ever change.

Finding the supposed right fit on paper is one thing, but translating that to the ice is something completely different. And yet McDavid continues to produce at a pace few can match, while adding to his already growing legacy. Last season brought us what was arguably the goal of the year against the Columbus Blue Jackets in his first game back from injury, that sent the entire hockey world into a frenzy. That was followed shortly thereafter by one of those so-called career-defining moments, albeit rather early in said career, torching the Toronto Maple Leafs for five points in his first meeting with the team he grew up cheering for.

Season two hasn't been much different, as the youngster has already put up three-point efforts on six separate occasions. One coming during the aforementioned head-to-head showdown with Crosby, and another accomplished by scoring his first-ever NHL hat trick against the Dallas Stars in mid-November. Ironically enough, the outburst came on the heels of a 10-game run in which McDavid managed to pick up seven assists but was unable to light the lamp for almost three full weeks.

"Three pretty lucky goals," McDavid said. "Said it yesterday, it's a funny league that way. You get Grade A chances, and they're not going in, then you start putting it there and they are going in. It's weird that way… definitely happy to get off that slump." Like most great players, he used that showing to help propel him to a nice little run. One that saw him score six times and put up 15 points over a seven-game stretch. No matter the era or player, the key to posting big numbers always includes a handful of hot runs over the course of a season.

At the end of the day, outside of Wayne Gretzky and Teemu Selanne, one could make the argument that the first 82 games of Connor McDavid's career were as good as any we have seen in history. Accomplishing what he has, in this era, and doing so while still a teenager is something that cannot be overstated, and it is a feather in the youngster's cap. As is the fact that he finds himself in a dead heat with Sidney Crosby and Evgeni Malkin atop the NHL scoring race before his 20th birthday. ∎

McDavid after scoring his first NHL career hat trick, in a game against the Dallas Stars on November 19, 2016, in Dallas.

Playoffs, Scoring Race, and Beyond

Forty-nine games doesn't make an NHL season, but from an Edmonton Oilers standpoint, the opening three months of their 2016–17 campaign could not have gone much better. With a little under a half-season's worth of games remaining on its schedule, this club sits third in its division with a 26–15–8 mark. That's right, the team that missed the playoffs for a 10th consecutive season in 2015–16 by finishing in the basement of the Western Conference with a mere 70 points and 31–43–8 record, is fighting tooth and nail with the Anaheim Ducks and San Jose Sharks for the Pacific Division crown.

It's hard to imagine, but when you take a closer look, it's not quite as surprising at it may seem. Cam Talbot has been superb to solid in almost every one his league-leading 43 appearances and has given his team a chance to win on a nightly basis. Veteran rear guard Andrej Sekera has been by far and away Edmonton's best defenceman, leading all blueliners in scoring with 21 points and time on ice at a hair under 22 minutes a night. Add to that the emergence of rookie Matthew Benning as a potential top-four guy, and the overall impact the additions of Adam Larsson and Kris Russell have had to the Oilers back end, and suddenly progress from one season to the next can be seen.

Leon Draisaitl has taken a major step forward in his second full-season in the NHL, becoming an offensive driver at even strength and on the man advantage. His 42 points make him a top 20 scorer in the league, and he has done yeoman's work in helping fill the void that was created with Taylor Hall's departure. Patrick Maroon continues to turn heads across the league, following up his strong finish over the final five-and-a-half weeks of 2015–16, with an eye-popping 18 goals on the season—all but two coming at even strength. All positive signs to be sure, but there is one crucial piece of the puzzle we have to get to.

From top to bottom, this is without question the most balanced roster we have seen from the Oilers in some time, but all of it hinges on one player. With all four of Jordan Eberle, Milan Lucic, Ryan Nugent-Hopkins, and Benoit Pouliot suffering through below- to well-below-average seasons, Edmonton has still managed to keep itself afloat, and much of that can be attributed to the play of Connor McDavid. As of January 24, 2016, the Richmond Hill native sits alone atop the league scoring leaders with 56 points on 16 goals and 40 assists, two points clear of the Pittsburgh Penguins' dynamic duo of Sidney Crosby and Evgeni

Connor McDavid in action in a 2–1 victory against the Calgary Flames on January 14, 2017, at Rogers Place in Edmonton.

McDavid fires a shot against the New Jersey Devils on January 7, 2017, in New Jersey, a 2–1 Oilers win in overtime.

Malkin, and eight points ahead of last season's most valuable player, Patrick Kane.

Not too shabby for a guy who until recently had played much of the year with two guys who have been fighting it all year long. With 11 goals on the season, it would be difficult to view Eberle's year as anything but a disappointment. While his point totals have only recently fallen off his career norms, almost all of it can be traced back to his inability to finish. At his current rate, the 26-year-old is on pace to finish the year with just 18 goals. To give that number some perspective, the Regina native has failed to score 24 goals in his NHL career on only two occasions. He had 18 goals in 69 games during his rookie campaign and 16 goals in 48 games in the lockout shortened 2012–13 season.

Safe to say Eberle hasn't suddenly forgot how to score goals, but for whatever reason, the puck isn't going in. Considering his career shooting average is 13.4 percent and he's sitting at 8.9 percent through 49 games this season, chalking it up to a combination of bad luck and a guy losing his mojo is a safe assumption. It happens to the best of them, but he may be showing signs of turning it around with a late-January surge of six points in four games. As for Lucic, it really has been a mixed bag of sorts. Typically, the veteran winger has been a strong even-strength producer and nothing to write home about on the man advantage through much of his career. But this season, the 28-year-old has been fairly productive on the power play and a non-factor on most nights at evens.

Like Eberle, chances are he will revert back to somewhere near his career average, but in the meantime, both have squandered numerous chances, and it has negatively impacted the club. Their lack of finish, combined with little to no offensive contribution from Nugent-Hopkins and Pouliot have likely cost the Oilers somewhere between five and seven points in

Edmonton fans celebrate an overtime goal by the Oilers' Connor McDavid in a 4–3 win against the Florida Panthers on January 18, 2017.

It seems as though whenever the gap has closed in the scoring race, McDavid wastes little time in doing something that would give him breathing room once again.

the standings. Add those to their current total of 60, and suddenly Edmonton would be right there with the Chicago Blackhawks and Minnesota Wild for the top spot in the conference. An opportunity missed, but one this group should still be able to overcome.

At the moment, the Oilers are a one-line show, as the trio of Draisaitl, Maroon, and McDavid have almost exclusively been keeping them afloat to start the New Year. Not exactly an ideal set-up but one certain teams can survive when they have a player who generates great scoring chance after great scoring chance on a nightly basis. Don't get me wrong, there have been evenings when McDavid hasn't been great over the course of the season, but those games are few and far between. Even on the nights when he is held off the scoresheet, the kid creates something and at the very least is handing the second and third lines far more favourable match-ups. But it's up them to do something with them.

No matter how you slice it, this group is about to enter uncharted territory. With a February schedule that will see the Oilers play nine of 12 games away from home, it is essential for the team to bank some points over the next week to give themselves a cushion to work with. Do that, and chances are quite good we will never again need to refer to the 2006 Stanley Cup Final run as the last time this organization made it to

the playoffs. With 13 of their final 18 games at Rogers Place, the playoffs should be nothing more than a foregone conclusion if they can take care of business on the road.

With 33 games left to go and a two-point cushion at his disposal, the chances of McDavid holding off the rest of the field to grab his first of what will likely be many a scoring title, are very real but by no means a sure thing. As deadly as his line has been of late, if the Oilers cannot find some kind of consistent secondary scoring threat over the course of the next few months, he will be hard-pressed to hold off the likes of Crosby, Malkin, and Kane, and the team could potentially fall out of playoff contention. On the other hand, it seems as though whenever the gap has closed in the scoring race, McDavid wastes little time in doing something that would give him breathing room once again.

Be it continuing to play alongside the combination of Draisaitl and Maroon or the reemergence of Eberle, you get the sense that McDavid is going to get a helping hand somewhere along the way, and that could be all he needs. Let's not forget that this isn't about going out and claiming that first Art Ross Trophy of his career, it's about getting the Edmonton Oilers back to the playoffs. Lucky for them, the chances of one occurring without the other are not very good—hence why my money would be on No. 97 every single time. ■

The Oilers' Darnell Nurse (25), Leon Draisaitl (29), Adam Larsson (6), and Connor McDavid (97) celebrate Draisaitl's goal against the Winnipeg Jets during the third period of a 6–3 Edmonton victory in Winnipeg on December 1, 2016.

Lowetide on No. 97

If you are a fan of the Edmonton Oilers, it is highly unlikely that you are unfamiliar with the name Allan Mitchell. Since starting his Lowetide blog back in 2005, Mitchell has been the heartbeat of the Oilers online community and is viewed as a pioneer of what is now known as the Oilogosphere. It was during Edmonton's surprising run to the 2006 Stanley Cup Final that his blog gained celebrity, thanks in large part to the posting of a "lucky" photo of former Oilers forward Stan Weir to help propel the ride.

Over the last decade-plus, the love affair between the Oilers fan base and Mitchell has only grown. On top of his own blog and contributions over at Oilers Nation, he hosts "The Lowdown with Lowetide" weekdays on TSN 1260 and continues to be a go-to source for all things involving the Orange and Blue. With that in mind, I thought it would be a heck of an idea to throw a few questions Mr. Mitchell's way about what the future might hold for one Connor McDavid.

Q: How much did Connor McDavid's arrival on the scene change the Edmonton Oilers long-term rebuild plans?

I think two things combined to change the organization's plans. First, the McDavid lottery…followed quickly by the addition of a veteran management/coaching group led by Peter Chiarelli and Todd McLellan. One does not happen without the other, but once the lottery

win occurred, in that instant everything was on the table in terms of trading assets and spending money. It truly was an enormous change in direction.

Q: Has there been an NHL player in recent memory who was anywhere close to as dominant as McDavid was during his rookie campaign in 2015–16?

You would probably have to go back to Crosby and Ovechkin a decade ago. The ice tilted when McDavid was on it, and that was an incredible sight to see. Players with this kind of ability to change the game every shift are extremely rare.

Q: Outside of Sidney Crosby, do you see any other current NHL player giving McDavid a run as the best player in the game in the here and now?

No. I think McDavid is already in the range with Crosby, and that is likely to continue until No. 97 is established as the premier player in the world. He really is that good.

Q: Can the Oilers leave McDavid and Leon Draisaitl on the same line over the long haul?

I think they can, but ideally Peter Chiarelli will provide his head coach with another strong option. As is the case with Evgeni Malkin in Pittsburgh, who can slide up as needed, having Leon as the second-line centre means Edmonton is going to give its opponents too much to handle

Connor McDavid looks locked-in during a game against the New Jersey Devils in January 2016.

McDavid attempts to score on Calgary Flames Goalie Brian Elliott in a game on January 14, 2017 at Rogers Place.

on most nights. Jesse Puljujarvi may be there in coming seasons.

Q: With minimal additions to the current roster, is it realistic to expect McDavid to carry this team to playoff success in the next two to three years?

Yes, but you would hope the general manager is looking to do more than have some postseason success. The idea is to win a Stanley Cup and even with McDavid on board, the club will need a flourishing farm system, better depth, and stronger balance in order to become a perennial contender.

Q: In order for McDavid to reach his full potential, is it critical for the organization to acquire a puck-moving horse on the back end?

I think they may already have one in Matt Benning, and also I believe one or both of Oscar Klefbom and Darnell Nurse could fit that bill. Not all of these men will turn into effective NHL puck movers, but there is some potential in this trio. So we may see the Oilers solve this issue internally.

Q: Where do you see McDavid's single-season point ceiling topping out at?

He is likely to push the 90–95-point plateau this season, and I imagine him hitting the century mark in 2017–18 or soon thereafter. It is nothing more than a wild guess at best, but I will say 120 points.

Q: Could the likes of an Auston Matthews or some other young player ultimately push McDavid for the "Best Player in the Game" moniker?

Too soon to tell… Matthews is getting a lot of play currently and does have a wide range of skills. It is honestly hard to imagine anyone pushing McDavid if he manages to remain healthy throughout his career. In several decades

McDavid warms up before his NHL debut, a road game against the St. Louis Blues on October 8, 2015.

"We are going to be able to chronicle and watch one of the greatest careers in hockey history unfold in front of our very eyes." —Allan Mitchell

watching hockey, I have never seen anyone make plays at such speeds. It is breathtaking.

Q: Is there any chance that McDavid could take a run at either one of Wayne Gretzky's Art Ross Trophy totals? Be it the seven straight he won as a member of the Oilers or 10 he won over the course of his extraordinary career.

I think those days are gone. I would think he will win multiple Art Ross Trophies, but winning seven straight in today's NHL seems next to impossible. Most teams are too close to equal, and poor teams can get better in a hurry via the draft and free agency. Gretzky won those awards (or most of them) with a collection of talent we will not see again in our lifetime.

Q: When the time comes and Connor McDavid retires from the game of hockey, do you think he will be mentioned in the conversation with the five players most consider to be the greatest of all-time (Wayne Gretzky, Bobby Orr, Gordie Howe, Mario Lemieux, and Maurice "Rocket" Richard)?

If he stays healthy, and adjusts his game over time, I believe that is his destiny.

It may be hard for some to accept, but like it or not, this is what this player is. Again, they don't come around that often, and in today's world of advanced technology and social media, we are going to be able to chronicle and watch one of the greatest careers in hockey history unfold in front of our very eyes. And with it will come an inordinate amount of scrutiny that no player before him has had to deal with, but this kid seems as ready for it as one could be.

"I just can't say enough good things about him, I just think he's such a special player," Gretzky said. "But he has everything in place to become the best player in the National Hockey League and go on to win some championships for the Edmonton Oilers. But listen, it's not going to happen overnight, it's hard to win, it's going to take time." Which is the beauty in all of this, as time is something he need not worry about. Simply put—continue doing what Connor McDavid does, and the rest should take care of itself. ∎

McDavid in action against the the New Jersey Devils in January 2016.

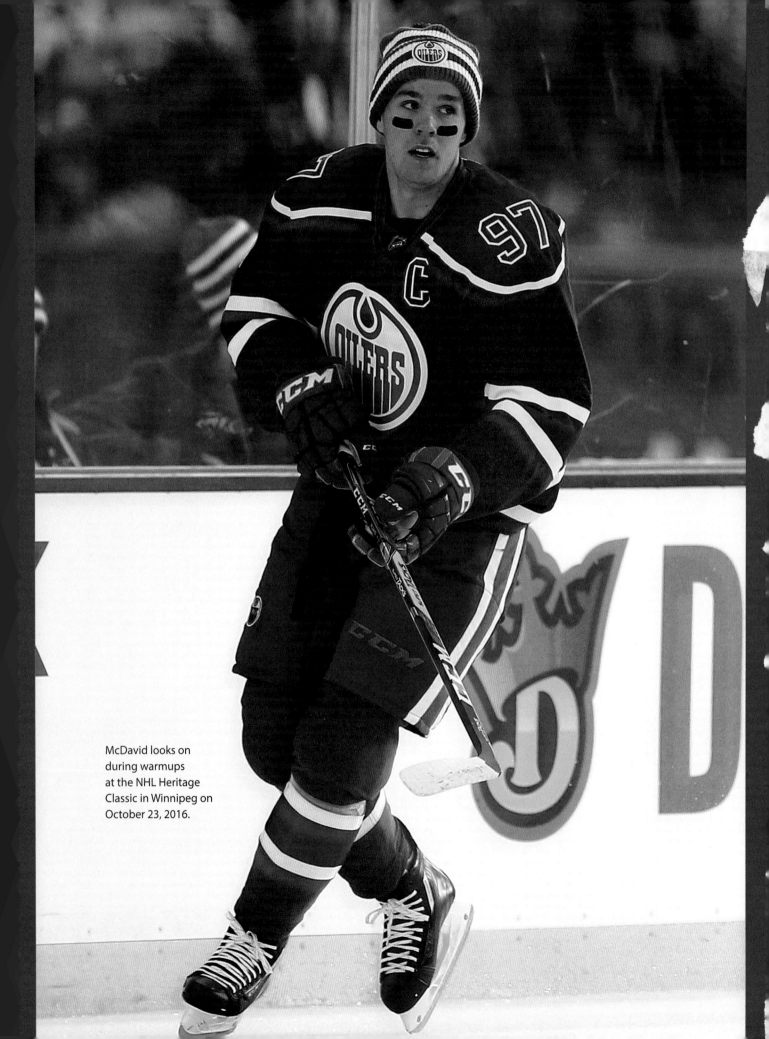

McDavid looks on during warmups at the NHL Heritage Classic in Winnipeg on October 23, 2016.